Infant
Swimming

Infant Swimming

The Gentle Water Play Method for Teaching Your Child to Swim

Cynthia Clevenger

St. Martin's Press
New York

This book is lovingly dedicated to the innocence of childhood and the joy of responsible parenting.

Design by Beth Tondreau

Library of Congress Cataloging-in-Publication Data

Clevenger, Cynthia.
    Infant swimming.

    1. Swimming for infants.   I. Title.
GV837.25.C57   1986   797.2'1'0880542
86-3687
ISBN 0-312-41594-X (pbk.)

First Edition

10 9 8 7 6 5 4 3 2 1

Contents

Acknowledgments

My deepest thanks are in order to Hobie Billingsley, the "Grandpa" of the Water Play program.

I would also like to thank Kathy Johnston, Linda Beale, and Gilda Yaw for encouraging my initial efforts in developing the Water Play program. Dianne Kobilca, Ben Lipton, and all the swimmers at Bulova Watch School in Queens, New York, taught me that mobility is the key to self-confidence.

Thanks to Parry Aftab-Caprio for her interest and invitation to conduct the Water Babies classes for the faculty and staff of the New York Hospital–Cornell Medical Center as a part of their Play Area Association programming.

Thanks to the three original babies in the program and their very supportive parents: Corey and Kim Cohen; Michelle, Ilene, and Peter Kadner; and Casey, Sheila, and Bill Davis. Manny Doran and "Uncle" Michael Kadner were extremely helpful in providing photographs and assorted art materials for the program. As an associate and instructor, Jeannie Dzurenko provided invaluable support and quality coaching time for many babies and their parents.

Arthur Anderson and Len Ruben deserve much praise for their sound legal counsel and undying support.

Anna, Susan, and Paul Tunick; Limi, Maiō, Camiā Rose, and Linda Perry; Kema, Maria, and Kevin Brabazon; Paul, David, Anu Graha, and Allen Ryshary; Mandy, Margi, Louise, and Bruce Smith; Nicholas, Anne, and Bob Early; Karen and Joe Faulkner and their daughters Stacy and Shelly gave me much spiritual encouragement and a more realistic scope for developing standards for the teaching of infant aquatics.

John Hutchins of The City of New York Department of Parks and Recreation deserves a big thanks for inviting the program to the Bath House pool in Harlem and providing help from his own staff members.

Dr. Richard Aslin, Dr. James ("Doc") Counsilman, and Wayne Oats I thank for their sponsorship of my individualized major in infant aquatics at Indiana University. Dr. Richard Young and Natalie Christophe deserve much credit for their exemplary program without which the Institute for Research in Infant Aquatics would have taken a great deal more time to develop.

The work of Sir Alister Hardy, Igor Tjarkovsky, Dr. Vladimir Guterman, Dr. Nicolai Bernstein, Dr. Edward T. Hall, Dr. Conrad Lorenz, and Dr. James E. Counsilman has been a constant source of inspiration as well as reference.

The work of Dr. Jack Bates, Dr. Gregory Pettit, Dr. Jeff Alberts, Dr. Esther Thelen, Dr. William Haeberle, and Judith Kladder has had a profound impact upon my work in infant aquatics. I sincerely hope that their influence is apparent and our association is just a beginning of creative collaboration.

The babies and parents who appear in this book made long treks to foreign cities to participate in community awareness programs such as the All Star Sports Health and Fitness Show, and to accommodate the photographer in two supplemental photo sessions. It is this dedication to long-term goals to which I have tried to pay due tribute. In appreciation I thank all the parents who have participated in the program over the years and who have helped to create a gentle, joyful home in the water for their children.

Photographs were taken at the Student Building Pool on the Bloomington campus of Indiana University, the Ramada Inn of Bloomington, and the Club House pool at Mohawk Hills in Carmel, Indiana.

Michael Neff deserves much credit for his artistic photographs of the babies in this book and his intuitive understanding of the babies' needs while photographing them in full underwater regalia.

I would like to thank Dr. Esther Thelen, Motor Development Specialist in the department of psychology at Indiana University, and Dr. Peter Scott, Pulmonary Pediatrician at Riley Children's Hospital for taking time from their busy schedules to edit this manuscript and clarify developmental and medical aspects of the program.

My very special thanks to my parents, Charlene and Bud Shropshire, and grandparents Karl and Lois Evarts for their support and encouragement over the years, and to Nat Sobel and Judith Weber who literally walked me through this first book because they experienced the benefits of the program with their daughter Anna Rachel, and to my very patient editor, Barbara Anderson, at St. Martin's Press in New York City.

Introduction

This book is written for parents who have newborns, infants, children age three to five, or exceptional babies. It is a summary of what I have learned from thousands of babies and their parents from all over the world using the Water Play approach, and what you should know before you first take your baby into the water. These exercises have developed over the years into the Water Play program that we use at Water Babies, Incorporated.

Ideally, you are the best coach for your baby's Water Play exercises. You know your baby's moods and the difference between a hungry cry or an unhappy cry. You know when she is pushing to try something new or holding back in apprehension. When you finish this book, you should have not only a step-by-step water exercise plan appropriate for your baby, but also an understanding of why it is important for your child to learn through play and to learn about swimming through the Water Play method.

You will learn what you can realistically expect your baby to accomplish in the water and you will have a clear understanding of your own expectations and how they will affect your baby's progress in the water.

You will also be able to create a secure and comfortable water environment for your baby at home in the tub or at the pool, and you will be able to make the best selection in choosing a class from local programs that are available to you.

Within these pages, you will learn how to read your baby's cues and how to respond to them in a fluid and rhythmic manner that conveys security. You will also learn how to hold and maneuver your baby in the water so that you both feel comfortable and confident. As you play together in the water, you will get to share in the joy of your baby's water discoveries and her early independence.

It doesn't matter if you have years of competitive swimming experience, or if you are fearful of water. Your expectations will change as you experience the Water Play method with your own child. My initial role as teacher has since become one of observer, dance partner, and environmental designer; just as yours will become. These roles are infinitely more fun because you are constantly learning, and infinitely more rewarding than that of just a teacher because you get to share in your baby's discoveries while you are fine-tuning your communication skills.

As an adult with years of athletic training, it has taken me a long time to change my own preconceived attitudes about the way babies swim. I thought babies would swim like adults—on their stomachs. But the babies taught me that swimming on the stomach was unnatural for them because their heads are so heavy. So, instead of trying to impose my standards upon the babies, I began to let their interests and natural abilities lead me.

You will encounter the same changes in attitude as your Water Play experiences evolve with your own baby. As you develop your own observational skills and practice the Water Play exercises that are supportive of your baby's interest, you will be better able to provide comfort, encouragement, and stimulation for your baby in the water. Infant swimming will then come to mean a great deal more to you than what you had originally expected, because these water skills can also be used on land, and that is when the fun begins!

Many parents who enroll in the Water Play classes are themselves fearful of the water and do not want their babies to grow up with that fear. Because the Water Play approach is based upon trust and security for both parent and baby, each parent and baby progresses as a team at their own level of comfort.

Working as a team is not only safer for baby, but many parents themselves grow comfortable while maneuvering in chest-deep water and begin to associate water with the joyful play times that they share with their babies. As their babies become independent and begin to swim distances, many parents enroll themselves in beginning swimming lessons just to keep up with their babies and discover that they no longer fear putting their own faces in the water or balk at the lessons!

So, no matter whether you are a competitive swimmer or fearful of water, the Water Play program can help you to understand better your baby's developing needs in water and show you how you can most effectively help your baby to reach his fullest Water Play potential—emotionally and intellectually as well as physically.

"If we could learn more playfully perhaps we wouldn't have to play so desperately."

—Marty Stouffer

1
Why Water?

Using Water to Enhance Mental and Motor Development

Most babies are born with sophisticated perceptual skills that they spend hours and years refining. Among these is the ability to perceive movement and patterns. Recently, this ability has become the interest of researchers worldwide. Results from a variety of research projects are giving us invaluable insight into just how "smart" our babies are.

Most people believe that language forms thought. But recent research by Michael Lewis of the Institute for Study of Exceptional Children in Princeton, New Jersey, has found that nonverbal infants can understand abstract ideas and are able to place objects in categories. In short, your baby can think even though he may not yet be able to speak or understand words.

Susan Rose and Wagner Bridger at Albert Einstein College of Medicine in New York have found that infants as young as six months can identify an object they, earlier, only touched through a screen. Rose believes the ability to make the connection between touch and vision may be the basis for symbolic thought and the creation of mental representations.

Psychologist Leslie Cohen of the University of Texas has found that even seven-month-old babies can recognize stuffed animals as being members of the same category. This "visual averaging" is thought to be the way babies generalize.

Clearly, we are just beginning to understand and appreciate infants' ability to think, to perceive, and to interact with the world around them. As research projects such as these further outline our babies' capabilities, we are better able to plan appropriate programs to enhance and develop our babies' natural talents. For example, we now know that after birth you can help enhance your baby's development by providing him with sensory stimulation and early movement experience, and water provides both. Water has a special feel—it's wet! It has a different temperature from the air, it smells different from air, it makes sound travel differently, and it makes objects in it and on it appear different than they do on land. Water stimulates all the senses, and because it provides a lessened field of gravity, it is a nearly perfect environment for your baby.

Early physical and mental stimulation is definitely helpful to your baby's development. Many parents even feel that their babies are smarter because of their early experience in water. While research is not yet conclusive, scientific studies are now suggesting connections between early motor stimulation, such as that involved in infant swimming, and emotional development in children.

Using Water to Enhance Parent/Baby Communication

Although early mental and physical stimulation is definitely helpful to your baby's development, parents also need to *respond* to their infants, helping their babies to be in control of their world.

Condon and Sander videotaped the body movements of infants on land, in response to adult speech. The tape played back in slow motion revealed that each infant made specific movements to specific consonants and vowels and that the infants repeated the same movement to the same sound again and again. Although this research has not yet been duplicated, Condon and Sander provided fascinating visual documentation of babies moving their bodies in response to their caregiver's voices. Your baby will also respond to your voice and actions with body movement.

Non-verbal movement communication is initially the only way your baby has of learning about you and his environment. So, your baby communicates and learns by moving his body and by repeating movements in different situations.

Body learning broadens into body language and seems to become incorporated into adult mannerisms. Body language varies from culture to culture, and should become the focus of much new research. George Lenard reports in his book *The Silent Pulse* that his researchers videotaped many conversations between different sets of two individuals. In slow replay, Lenard found that body movements of the two conversationalists actually looked like a dance, the listener responding rhythmically to the body movements of the speaker.

Tension arose when the conversationalist's movements were not harmonious, as when both partners moved forward or backward at about the same time.

In the water you can observe your baby's body learning by observing the smoothness of the baby's water movements and the rhythm that you share in communicating in the water. You will notice that your baby's body language with your spouse is in a completely different tempo. Although there will be common movements that you all will share, your water communication with your baby will be completely unique in rhythm and tempo.

Body learning, individually or as part of a team, is by far the single most important reason for your baby to experience water. In learning to maneuver your bodies in the water, you and your baby are actually learning another language of movement. By learning to speak this language with another person, you broaden your own sense of self and your communication skills.

Because cultural body mannerisms are drastically modified in the water, body communication in water, like that of an astronaut's in space, is truly a universal language. So, when you first create an inviting water environment for your baby and then learn to speak to each other in body language, your baby will learn that you will respond in harmony to his needs in the water and that he can trust you. Learning to trust is recognized by child development experts as a major developmental milestone, and should be the foundation for all learning experiences.

Using Water to Help Baby Relax

Every parent has at one time or another resorted to the rocking chair to calm a fussy baby. Rocking will soothe and calm an unhappy child; older babies instinctively rock to comfort themselves. Rocking stimulates your baby's vestibular system (the area in the inner ear that tells you whether you are right side up or upside down). We all like vestibular stimulation, like riding on a roller coaster or bouncing on a trampoline, but rather than being stimulated by rocking, we find it to be calming and relaxing. Just sleeping on tiny water beds has helped prematurely born infants, who, because of underdeveloped nervous systems, exhibit disorganized movements, fragmented sleep patterns, and excessive irritability that make them difficult to care for. Dr. Anneliese Korner, Professor of Psychiatry and Behavioral Medicine at the Stanford University School of Medicine uses incubator water beds that have gentle head to foot motions for pre-term babies. Two different studies revealed that premature babies placed on these water beds have fewer occasions of breathing interruptions (apnea). The experimental groups were also found to demonstrate significantly more mature motor behavior and fewer signs of irritability.

Swimming babies, once independent in the water, like to just "hang in suspension," with their arms and legs completely relaxed. Even passing toys cannot entice them to move; buoyancy sensations and gentle rocking offer their own rewards.

Your baby's breathing will affect her level of buoyancy in the water. Independent little ones discover this very early and need lots of free time to experiment with their breathing—to bob in the water and experience the different sensations caused by having the lungs filled with different amounts of air. This early form of breath control should help increase your baby's oxygen intake and build respiratory and muscular endurance, while helping your baby to work off energy.

Mothers often tell me that even after the first water class, their babies eat better and sleep more deeply. One mother sighed and explained that her baby's nap time on swimming days was twice as long and that this was the first opportunity she had to read a book since the baby was born, eight months earlier.

Babies need help to discharge excess energy. What better way than through touch and movement in an environment that is conducive to movement—water.

The Water Play Approach

The Water Play approach is the safe way to help your baby learn to swim. Working as a team, your water adaptation will gently progress from stages of adjusting to the temperature of the water (as you both first enter the water) to adjusting to the buoyancy of your bodies in the water. As balance steadies, your baby will move into early levels of independent swimming. As the caregiver in the water, your role is to "read" your baby's cues.

As you practice slowing your movements to adjust to the resistance of the water, they will develop a fluid rhythm. Communication between you and your baby will then develop into a distinct and unique "dance," which can be as easily observed as your baby's physical development in water. The quality of your water dancing will, to a certain extent, reflect your and your baby's progress in the water. On bad days, you will realize that you are out of synch.

The water-dancing exercises are designed to build your own ability to aid and maneuver your baby in the water, while at the same time encouraging your baby's independence and self-confidence.

As you observe your baby in the water, your attitude toward his progress will develop from a genuine sense of joy at every little achievement to a growing appreciation of your baby's individual accomplishments and developing personality. Babies learn through exploration and self-discovery and can be lovingly guided to independence, without a trace of trauma.

The Water Play program evolves around the understanding that water is a wonderful medium and that we want to share our enjoyment of it with others. We cannot share enjoyment if the very thing we enjoy causes another person fear or discomfort. You will be there not to "teach" your baby swimming skills, but to create and communicate a secure environment that your baby will want to explore to its fullest.

Within the water environment, your baby will actually use you as a base for physical comfort and support. If your baby trusts from previous experience that she will receive comfort from you whenever there is a need, she will have the security and growing self-confidence to leave you and explore the water environment in ever widening circles.

Through exploration and self-discovery, your baby's adaption to water will develop naturally. You will be there to love and encourage your baby by offering new situations. But your baby will decide what she wants to accept and what she wants to share. Playful attitudes develop from being comfortable and secure in the water and in trusting one another to respond harmoniously in your water dancing.

From the Water Play viewpoint, what is most important is the development of the inner self-confidence that comes of making water a second home and a happy place to play. Water skill acquisition occurs then quite naturally, no matter at what age you begin. For this reason, the Water Play program can be directly applied and suitably modified to individuals of all ages and of all physical capabilities. Although an infant represents almost unlimited human potential, when you think about it, who is more limited in physical ability than an infant? So, even the individual with severe mental or physical disabilities can learn to adapt comfortably to water and gain a very personal sense of confidence and self-mastery through the Water Play philosophy and skill exercises.

2
When and Where to Begin

Your pediatrician will let you know when your newborn is ready for his first bath and whether or not you should get his ears wet. Swimming in a public pool can expose your newborn to a variety of germs and bacteria and is not recommended until after the first round of immunization shots, or at about three months of age. Most programs now ask for a medical release form from your pediatrician before enrolling you. It is a good practice and alerts your pediatrician to look for swimming-type ailments, such as ear infections.

Parents with a swimming pool at home can begin the program as soon as the umbilical stump has completely healed. Again, check with your pediatrician. If you are in a great hurry to begin, you may be rushing things a bit. One small infection can keep your baby out of the water for weeks, so it is worth waiting an extra day or two.

Healthy water is crucial to your baby's well-being. If your pool cannot be heated to a minimum of 86° F, if you cannot keep constant water readings, or if you do not have a swimming pool, you can begin at home in the sink or tub.

Creating an Enjoyable Bath Experience

Bathtime rituals vary from family to family and from culture to culture. Because your baby's tactile and inner ear senses are highly developed before birth, these are the two most important factors to consider when giving your baby a bath at home. Your baby's vision begins to develop after birth, and by the end of the second month, most all babies have developed a sensitivity to brightness. So, water and air temperature, sound as well as light, will be the areas you need to concentrate on making comfortable and reassuring for your baby.

Warmth

Locate the coziest water room in the house. Bathrooms are usually smaller than kitchens, and air temperature can be more easily regulated. Removing warm clothes and exposing your baby to air that is even five degrees cooler than your baby's skin temperature can be uncomfortable, and colder air or drafts can even hurt. Water that is splashed over baby's body draws off body heat quickly, making baby even more uncomfortable. So you want to create a physically comfortable environment and avoid drafts and cold.

At one time or another, you will probably bathe baby in the kitchen sink, the bathtub, and the shower. You can begin each bath by some preliminary planning. Shut the windows and doors and draw baby's bathwater or turn on the shower for a few minutes to warm the air and moisten it. Some bathrooms have their own wall heaters that you can use even during cold and rainy summer days.

Music

Find a safe place away from your bathing area and plug in a tape recorder that will give you at least one-half hour of continuous music. Choose relaxing and soothing music for bedtime and a faster tempo for a morning bath. Music should help set the stage for an enjoyable bathtime and not become the main sensory experience, so do not play it too loud and do not have too much bass.

Dr. Steven Halpern in his book *Sound Health* mentioned the *sound* research of Dr. Theodore D. Wacks at Purdue University. His research found that babies who lived in noisy homes were slower to imitate adult behavior and exhibited delayed verbal development and exploratory activity.

Dr. Halpern also points out that pop music played even in fitness centers employs the stopped-anapestic rhythms that research has shown *weakens* muscles. Pop music can actually throw off muscular coordination and confuse the brain.

Because we want to create an environment that is *supportive* of muscular coordination and exploratory activity, you'll want to carefully select music for your baby's water and land environments.

When the music is on, and the lighting is soft and indirect, you can bring baby into the room so that she has a few minutes to adjust to the change of air temperature and humidity. Be sure to pull the door shut behind you as you enter and leave or you will lose all that warm, moist air.

Warming the Tub

When tea is served in the Orient, the brewing pot and the cups are warmed by hot water before the tea is poured into them, otherwise the pot and cups draw heat from the liquid, cooling the tea. In drawing your baby's bath, you will want to warm the porcelain or metal of your sink or tub by letting warm water stand in it for a few minutes. By pouring water over the areas of the sink not submerged, you can warm the entire area. Remember what a surprise it is to lean back against a cold tub after sitting awhile in steamy water.

There are any number of bathing tubs or pads to place in the sink or tub for baby's bath. You can also set most plastic carriers down in the water. An inexpensive pad for babies who are not yet standing is a stack of folded terry cloth towels. The water will weight them down and keep cold metal, tile, or porcelain from contact with baby's skin. Wetted towels can also be draped over the side of the tub and periodically remoistened to keep them warm. (Towels should not be used for children who can pull themselves up and stand because it is too easy to slip.)

Bath Materials

Have all bath materials such as shampoo, soap, and toys, and all after-bath items such as towels, powder, and diapers close at hand. This will keep you at your baby's side during the entire bathtime. Many parents keep their bath materials in their swim bags and can tote all bath goodies from one room to another, or to Grandma's on a moment's notice, without forgetting a thing.

Expect to Get Wet!

Most bath frustrations can be eliminated if you set realistic expectations of your baby's water progress and allow adequate time for play as well as getting clean. But most of all, expect to get wet!

The more active your baby, the greater amount of splashed water you can expect. Invariably, water will be everywhere. Keep a mop handy and hang on to those fraying or fading towels. You can place them around the sink or tub areas to help absorb the deluge.

Sitting and splashing in a sink or tub of water can be great fun. Babies learn that water is a responsive plaything, that unexpected water in the eyes and face, although always a surprise, is not threatening. Babies six months to two years of age can sit securely in a bathtub helper seat with a foam cushion. Four large suction cups anchor the Baby Sitter™, while a plastic ring provides back and hand support. Infants too young to hold their heads erect and to sit can practice backfloats (see Chapter 7).

By climbing into the tub with your little one, you can open up a whole new world of possibilities. With your help, your baby can sit, stand, and float. If you want to shower before climbing into the tub, then you can also practice licking the water and bubbles together.

Most of the "Hands On" and "Hands Off" maneuvers can be adapted to the tub. Depending upon your size in relationship to the size of the tub, practice what you can comfortably in the amount of space that you have. You can save activities requiring more space for the pool.

Soaping Up

Soaping up should always *follow* your water play. Soapy water can sting eyes, and bubbles popping in your baby's ears can be frightening. Drinking soapy water can cause your baby digestive and elimination problems, so take extra time to let baby play in the water before soaping up. Bathtime should be mostly fun, with a quick but thorough soaping at the end.

Rinsing Off

You can rinse your baby by pouring fresh warm water from a plastic cup over the back of the head and shoulders. To rinse the face, tip baby's head forward and pour from the back of the head. No matter whether your baby is upright or lying on her back, never pour water directly onto her face. Water poured on the face gets into the eyes and can cause your baby to hold her breath momentarily. It can also force water up into the nostrils and sinuses and it stings a lot. In general, babies just do not like it, and that should be enough.

Never rinse baby off underneath the faucet. Running water splashing into a baby's personal space is frightening, and you also run the risk of scalding baby. It takes only one second of exposure to 156° F water to produce a third-degree burn. You can use a cooking thermometer to check on the hot water temperature.

Scaldings can be prevented by turning the hot water heater down to 120° F. Metal faucets and spouts can also cause burns, so push those aside or cover them during bathtime. Sassy's® Bathing Safety Kit includes a cushioned spout guard and non-skid safety treads for the tub or sink.

Massage

Rubdowns after a warm bath are especially nice. Warm the oil in your hands before you place it on baby, or drop the *plastic* bottle in the bath water to warm. Place baby on a clean, dry towel. Relax your hands and let them do the thinking. Continue to reach for dry spots until baby is thoroughly oiled and then scoop baby up in the towel and buff him dry.

Hot Tubs

After a good workout or at the end of an exhausting day, nothing sounds better than a long soak at the club or at home in a hot tub. Babies cannot throw off heat as adults can and are even more susceptible to heat exhaustion than we are. Even adults often overdo a hot tub routine and it is common lifeguard training at clubs to watch the hot tubs for fainting adults.

Although most little ones understand what "hot" is to touch, they cannot communicate to an adult that their body is "too hot" because a hot body is a new sensation. Infants are at the greatest risk in a hot tub or whirlpool because their metabolisms are different from ours, and because free chlorine combines and evaporates rapidly, allowing bacteria and other living things to multiply in the primordial soup of a hot tub. For these reasons, hot tubs are not recommended Water Play areas.

3
What You Can Expect Your Baby to Learn

Infants have very different land interests and capabilities than do toddlers, and toddlers have vastly different skills from older preschool children.

This chapter will help you understand your child's land and water capabilities at various stages. Each baby will take his own interest and abilities into the water. The nice thing about water is that anything that you try to do on land is easier in the water because the water supports the weight of the body. The very strength that your infant has worked for months to develop on land is a natural given in the water. By taking advantage of this wonderful opportunity, you can actually help your infant to sit, stand, and walk, so that he can get on with exploring his universe.

Infants from Birth to Walking

Even infants from birth to walking have different interests and capabilities. They move from initial reflexive movements into movements that they themselves can awkwardly direct. Postural control begins with the head, and by the fourth to sixth month, most infants cannot only hold the head erect but also sit if propped against a supportive surface. Between the sixth and the ninth months, infants begin to scoot and crawl and then to pull themselves up and stand. By the tenth to the twelfth month, most infants can walk with helping hands or by holding onto furniture.

In the water, you can work on exercises that will help your baby's land development. Back floats and stability exercises that help baby strengthen muscles that control his head and sitting and standing postures will be the most fun. You can help by using the "Hands On" maneuvers (see Chapters 5 and 6).

Infants have the distinct advantage of having no fear of water. Some become so comfortable that they can actually fall asleep while floating on their backs, while mother beams proudly in amazement, just within arm's reach.

Infant Reflexes

All infants are born with reflexive movement patterns such as rooting, sucking, and grasping. Each infant will acquire each reflex in varying strengths according to genetic makeup. Individual genetic structure will also determine the length of time that the reflex is controlled by the brain stem.

These early reflexes seem to "disappear" after a few months. Some of the movement patterns of the early reflexes then again seem to "reappear" later in development, incorporated into more sophisticated movements that your baby performs voluntarily, if awkwardly at first.

Researchers do not yet understand the connections between reflexes, their stages of disappearance, and the reappearance of voluntary movements. One possibility is that the control of movements is shifting from one area of the brain, the brain stem, to another, the cerebral cortex, the origin of voluntary movements. It stands to reason, however, that with any switch of authority in a hierarchical system, there is often a breakdown of familiar communication channels, and a *period of time* is necessary for restructuring and translating old information into the language that the new authority understands.

A second possibility is that the pattern of movements of the early reflexes is itself breaking up, so that your baby can use her limbs in more complex ways. This means that the baby will not be so "locked" into a fixed pattern of responding.

A third possibility is that other systems developing in the infant may mask or interfere with the reflex patterns. These may involve maturing posture and balance, changes in muscle strength, or simply changes in what the baby is paying attention to. For example, although the stepping response disappears at about two months, infants will still make vigorous kicking movements when on their backs, suggesting that posture may influence movments. Whatever the underlying cause, however, it seems clear that infants seem to have periods when they appear less well organized than at an earlier age, but we believe these periods are necessary for further development.

Reflexes that operate on land are also operable in water. There are two reflexes that most infant aquatic programs place a great deal of emphasis upon training—the swimming reflex and the mammalian diving reflex.

THE SWIMMING REFLEX

The swimming reflex involves rhythmical extensor and flexor movements of your infant's arms and legs and can be observed by holding your infant (supporting the baby's head) over water in a prone position. Developmental theorist Myrtle McGraw believes that the swimming reflex is a precursor to crawling and is associated with walking.

Sir Alister Hardy, an eminent British marine biologist, and Igor Tjarkovsky, a Russian researcher, believe that the waving and kicking motions that newborns and older babies make are actually tiny swimming motions.

The inhibition phase of the swimming reflex, the period during which the reflex disappears, is generally recognized to occur between the third and sixth months. This, of course, varies from infant to infant, but can be readily observed by noting the changes in the infant's swimming movement pattern. The once-coordinated and rhythmic strokes with both arms and legs will become disoriented and change to uncoordinated thrashing movements.

In a near vertical position, shoulders in the water, it is interesting to note that most babies reflexively use only the torso, legs, and feet for kicking. Only after a rhythmic bicycle kick is established (voluntary control) and can be used for forward locomotion, with the body angling forward in the water, do the arms stretch forward as if to press down upon the water for balance. Stroking the water develops naturally from this "pressing."

THE MAMMALIAN DIVING REFLEX

The mammalian diving reflex of newborns is a complicated and much misunderstood reflexive movement pattern. Researchers who study the reflex do not themselves understand it fully. The reflex is not easily observed because it occurs during submersion of the face in water. The time that this reflex disappears is thought to occur between the third and sixth months.

Tjarkovsky believes that the first twelve hours after birth is the most critical time for stimulating the reflex for water operability, and it is reported that at two weeks of age Tjarkovsky's water-trained babies can reflexively hold their breath under water for two minutes or longer.

This is very exciting information, but the important thing to understand during your Water Play exercises is that Tjarkovsky's babies train several hours per day, while your baby will be in water just a few hours per week.

Babies cannot be expected to "learn" a movement pattern such as breath holding until they have gained voluntary control over the pattern. The high incidence of "forgetting" that occurs in drownproofing classes suggests that stimulus-response training methods need to be restructured to accommodate each baby's developmental needs. Tjarkovsky's babies begin water training at birth, when the diving reflex is strongest, and only qualified medical professionals work with the infants. Parents also attend many weeks of classes to prepare for this work.

In the United States, we enroll our babies in aquatics programs during their third month, at the earliest, at just about the time the diving and swimming reflexes begin to wane and then go "underground." So, stimulus-response training of these reflexes is inappropriate for most babies older than three months. Parents whose babies are enrolled in an infant aquatics class are there to learn and have little or no preparation. They learn by trial and error as they go, which is risky at best.

Training programs for babies under three months of age that intend to train the diving and swimming reflexes should be handled by qualified medical professionals, preferably in a hospital setting. These programs should include preparation and water adjustment classes for parents before water work begins.

OTHER REFLEXES TO LOOK FOR

While your baby may be too old to practice stimulus-response training of the swimming and diving reflexes, she's just in time to make use of water to achieve her motor milestones! Put into perspective, the diving and swimming reflexes are just two of the many reflexes that you can observe and then learn to elicit with the Water Play exercises. Exercising any of the reflexes will help your baby build muscular strength.

The sucking and rooting reflexes can be elicited by stroking your infant's cheek with a finger. She will turn her head toward the pressure, and the sucking reflex will begin as her mouth closes over your finger.

When your baby's chin and lips get wet in the water, she will also reflexively turn toward the pressure or tickle of the water and begin to make sucking motions. Your baby will also imitate your licking the water and will attempt to blow bubbles.

The labyrinth-righting reflex can be elicited by placing baby on her back in the water while supporting the head. The chin will come forward to the chest and the knees will draw up toward the chest. Similarly, if you place your baby on her tummy in the water, supporting her head above the water surface, this reflex will cause your baby to try and keep her head upright by arching the back, and lifting her head.

The moro reflex can also be observed during back floats in the water. As your baby's head is gently lowered back into the water, the arms and legs will flex and draw up in almost a fetal position. The moro reflex can also be observed when you pull your baby into the water from a higher deck surface. The moro reflex disappears between the third and fourth month.

The palmer grasp reflex can be observed in the water by placing your baby's hands over the lane line or gutter line of the swimming pool. You can also let her grasp your fingers as you pull her forward through the water. The grasp reflex disappears between the third and fourth month.

Pull-up reactions of the arms can be observed by letting your baby sit or stand in your lap while grasping your fingers. As you move your hands backward or forward your baby will flex one or both arms at the elbow to keep her balance.

The crawling reflex can be elicited on land by placing baby on her tummy and alternately applying pressure to the soles of her feet. The arms and legs will move together in a crawling pattern. In the water, this reflex is indistinguishable from the swimming reflex. The crawling reflex disappears between the third and fourth month.

The stepping or walking reflex can be observed by supporting your infant in an upright position and moving her slightly forward and from side to side. She will begin to make a high-stepping motion, the hip, knee, and ankle flexing at about the same time. The stepping or walking reflex disappears between the second and third month.

The supporting reflex of the arms kicks in at about the fourth month and can be observed when you lower baby horizontally into the water. Your baby will extend her arms in an attempt to brace herself on the surface of the water.

The climbing reflex will begin sometime around the twelfth month and remain for sometime into the second year. In the water this reflex can be observed after an accidental dunking, as baby climbs up your torso as though you were a tree.

A WORD OF CAUTION

We don't really know if early stimulation of a reflex will strengthen it to the point that it will remain with the child through the reflex's normal stage of inhibition. In water this means that a two-month-old infant may be able to perform reflexively necessary survival skills, but at six months he cannot, because these reflexes are no longer operating.

Drownproofing training, although it might be appropriate for infants with breath-holding reflexes (it is extremely difficult to determine if this reflex is operating), is inappropriate and possibly dangerous for those infants whose reflex has phased into the inhibition stage.

Should your baby be under four months of age, and should you be extremely comfortable in water and really want to work with your baby on stimulating the diving reflex, here are a few words. First of all, absolutely no one, not even an adult, can be drownproofed, and secondly, over the years I have found that television and the current interest in the human potential movement have popularized the idea of the diving reflex with such slogans as "All babies come from water" and "It's natural, every baby can hold his breath under water."

Although every baby has the potential for becoming a swimmer, the methods that you use in working with your baby will be crucial to his health, as well as his well-being. That means you will want to do some homework. Please read Chapter 4, "Reading Your Baby's Cues," and Chapter 10, "Medical Considerations," and have several water weeks together before you begin any underwater work.

You will not have been acquainted with your baby for any great length of time, and his behavior will change from month to month. Being able to respond promptly to your baby's underwater cues is extremely important. So, if you have not had an opportunity to work closely with a number of infants (in a hospital, for example), getting acquainted with your little one on land will take time, so you will want to take extra time in water.

Walking to Two-Year-Olds

Children who are beginning to walk—to take independent steps on land—are interested in independence in water as well. Water time for this group is best spent with "Hands Off" maneuvers (see Chapter 7) and the equipment that your baby is already familiar with. Flippers add body length to help stabilize balance; walls, ladders, and floating objects can be used for balance much like the coffee table at home. Tubie suits and other flotation suits will provide additional buoyancy, but must fit your baby properly to be of benefit.

Two- to Three-Year-Olds

Two- to three-year-olds will acquire rough balance and buoyancy skills quickly and move into experimenting with direction of their movement. Once independent locomotor skills enable your baby to direct her movement in the water, her concentration is free to attend to other interests and to explore beyond old boundaries.

Three- to Five-Year-Olds

Three- to five-year-olds or preschoolers who have had prior water experience are usually quite confident and happy in water.

These children can begin additional breathing exercises and stroke technique. Because this group is taller, they can use the spine as a lever to lift their head from the water to breathe. When breath control is relatively effortless, your little one will usually become interested in underwater exploration. Talking babies seem to discover one another in the water and these new social contacts encourage further refinement of locomotor movement while an interest in speed of directional movement develops.

Preschoolers who are uncomfortable in water or who are reluctant to try new exercises should remain with water-adjustment exercises until they are confident and show an interest in further exploration.

Exceptional Babies

Exceptional babies from birth to five years will follow the same developmental sequences that all babies follow, except at a slower pace. Severe limitations may halt development at a given point for some time, but swimming, whether it be early motor stimulation or a maintenance exercise, is a highly rewarding experience for both parent and baby. All babies are gravity-bound, and water allows each little one a full range of free motion. This freedom is exhilarating, and the exceptional baby's physical progress is easily observed and greatly encouraging.

The lessening of gravity in the water and the tactile pressures of the water itself will offer some initial confusion for older babies, preschoolers, and exceptional babies. We learn about feet and hands by the way that they "feel" in relation to the rest of our body.

In the water, the sensory signals that tell your little one where her feet are located will be completely different. Toddlers and preschoolers who are walking are already aware of their feet and body postures on land because they "feel" a certain way. In the water, everything will "feel" different and it is not uncommon for these "land-oriented" babies to think that their bodies have disappeared.

The same land movement will feel different in water to you as well as to your baby, so no matter what age your baby begins Water Play exercises, you always want to begin with postural exercises that will let your baby rediscover her hands and feet as well as her new balance in water.

What About Water Safety?

All parents want their preschoolers to be safe in and around water. Certainly, water experience will give your baby the opportunity to develop basic water skills, but you cannot waterproof your baby or make him drownproof.

Realistically, happy water encounters will enhance your baby's interest in water, so you will need to take extra precautions. Your baby's life experiences and reasoning powers are limited, but his curiosity is boundless. To place even one percent of water safety responsibilities upon little shoulders is a life-and-death gamble.

Babies need a warm and inviting environment. You can create a safe and secure water environment for your baby by making simple changes that will then allow you to focus your attention completely upon your baby and your Water Play exercises. Rather than placing false trust in your baby's swimming abilities, you will have greater peace of mind by securely enclosing your pool or fencing in your yard. To break up the monotony of an afternoon of lifeguarding, team up with friends and switch with another parent or two so that your children have constant and alert supervision.

Will Water Play Exercises
Drownproof My Baby?

Everyone has at one time or another seen a TV program demonstrating drownproofing for babies. Babies are "trained" by forced immersions to hold their breath and roll over on their backs. This training must be done to the baby, and generally begins by having the baby dropped into the water from the deck. The trainer then initiates a series of rolls and turns until the baby can eventually right himself and float on his back unaided. The training is available for young infants as well as for older preschool children. I, personally, do not recommend drownproofing or waterproofing techniques. The term itself is misleading, causing many parents to feel overconfident of their child's water abilities, and the babies I have observed in these classes always scream—not just cry, but scream. They seem to be terrified and fighting for their very lives. Those cries go unanswered for quite lengthy stretches of time so that the babies can learn to stay afloat while crying. Because I learned to follow my intuition while working with babies, I believe there is something wrong with this approach. My reasoning is that this approach does not encourage sensitive communication between parent and child in the water. So parents and babies miss out on this wonderful experience together.

What's the Difference Between a Drownproofing Program and the Water Play Program?

Drownproofing classes remove the baby from the parent to teach water survival skills. Water Play classes teach the parents how to observe and work with their children and to supplement their developmental interests in water.

Water survival skills, such as forced immersions, taught in drownproofing programs are "done to" the baby or imposed upon her. Water Play exercises, such as standing in the hands, are *offered to* the babies and if the infant is apprehensive or unable to perform, she is allowed to choose what she wants to do from several different options.

Parents in the Water Play program develop a very realistic understanding of their babies' capabilities in the water because they are in the water with the babies.

What's the Difference Between Other Water Learning Programs and the Water Play Program?

All water learning programs work with the parent and baby together. But most water learning programs have a set format of exercises to perform on day one, day two, etc. Often these exercises are not developmentally appropriate for the age of the child. Most water learning programs also use drownproofing techniques such as forced immersions and blowing in the face to stimulate the diving reflex. Water Play exercises don't mix techniques and are designed in steps so that babies and their parents will be comfortable with a given skill before advancing to the next skill. Water Play exercises are developmentally appropriate for each baby because we let the babies make their own choices. The Water Play program promotes the verticle swimming position, which most other water learning programs don't recognize.

The Water Play program strives for consistency in nonverbal communication between parent and baby and is the only program that has choreographed water-dancing exercises.

Realistic Water Milestones

Although your baby's age will influence his water capabilities, it does not matter at what age your baby learns a water skill. What is important is that your baby learn them in sequence.

With a swimming aid and then without one your baby should:

1. Feel comfortable in the water in your arms.
2. Make the decision to leave the security of your arms.
3. Learn the vertical body position (initially, this can be performed only with your help).
4. Develop the respiratory strength to build self-confidence through control of buoyancy.

5. Be able to balance with two-hand holds.
6. Be able to balance with a one-hand hold.
7. Be able to balance while independently buoyant.
8. Develop forward movement with *any* kicking and stroking pattern.

Your little one can begin these exercises at any age, but he should start at the beginning of the series. Older babies will, of course, run through the series more quickly than younger babies.

Your baby will creatively work to acquire these skills and may spend two days at one skill and be able to perform it fairly efficiently, while it may take him three months to perform another. It does not matter. Each baby should take just as much time as he needs. So much more is going on with your baby emotionally and intellectually, that assessing your baby's development just by his physical progress will not give you a fair picture. So relax your expectations, get wet, and enjoy your baby in the water.

4
Reading Your Baby's Cues

B efore you first get into the water, there are several cues that your baby will give you that you should be familiar with. We are only just beginning to understand and fully appreciate the complex social needs of babies. While babies cannot yet express their needs and feelings through speech, they do have other ways of communicating. Most babies give out clear emotional signals, and it is up to us to "read" these signals and respond appropriately. Growing evidence shows that parents who are responsive and sensitive to their baby's emotional cues have babies who are characteristically more secure and show greater interest in exploring their environment, whether it be on land or in water.

Sensitive parenting in the Water Play program involves responding to your baby's signals promptly and effectively. These signals usually take the form of looking (photo 4.1), smiling, and seeking physical contact (photo 4.2). In the water, you and your baby will initially be facing one another at eye level. With the intensity of almost constant face-to-face interaction, your baby will frequently have to take a break. She will communicate this need for rest simply by breaking eye contact and turning her head away (photo 4.3).

4.1. A quizzical look will let you know that you need to move more slowly and deliberately in handling your baby in the water.

4.2. Parents who "read" their babies' "cues" will seldom have tearful babies in the water.

4.3. Even contented babies need to break eye contact and often turn the head as well. Thumb- or handsucking is a sure sign that your little one needs a break.

Parents often try to recapture baby's interest by increasing the level of playful stimulation by tickling baby, or by turning her so that eye contact is reestablished. But it is more effective in the long run to relax and wait until baby signals a readiness to continue playing with you, by catching your eye again (photo 4.4).

4.4. When your baby is ready to resume play, he will reestablish eye contact with you.

Baby's "OK"

All babies, like older children, will signal their joy and interest in a water activity by smiling at you (photo 4.5). This is to let you know that they are having a good time and want to continue. Baby's "OK" is easy to pick up on since almost everyone is captivated by a smiling baby.

4.5. Both Nicholas and his mother are enjoying this water game.

When your baby cries, it is important to respond promptly, eliminating the source of distress, while providing comfort. This source may be obvious—such as getting water in the eyes (photo 4.6) or bumping a chin—or it may be a mystery. What is very clear, however, is that your baby is unhappy and needs loving support and physical comfort from you (photo 4.7). By recognizing your baby's physical need for comfort and by responding without delay, you are helping your baby to establish a secure "base" from which all future exploration and learning will build. When your baby has had enough reassurance to again feel confident, he will indicate his readiness to resume play by turning to you and giving you the "OK" smile as he begins to reach away from you, or as he begins to study another person, toy, or activity (photo 4.8).

4.6. Left: Water in the eyes and ears tickles and is initially uncomfortable.

4.7. Below left: Eliminate the problem and hold your little one close until you get the "OK" with a smile.

4.8. Below right: Besides a smile, interest in a toy or another activity is also a sure sign that your little one is ready for play.

Fear

Your baby will signal uncertainty and fearfulness by seeking to be near you or by trying to maintain physical contact with you. While occasionally inconvenient or even embarrassing for you, as her parent, this contact is essential if baby is to learn that she is safe (photo 4.9).

4.9. Lynn's mother uses close contact and an even tone of voice to calm and comfort Lynn's apprehension. A big hug and a little pat go a long way.

Older children who are more land experienced are often more frightened by water than babies. Should your baby be fearful of the water, no amount of reasoning or shaming can ease that fear (as any fearful adult can explain), because fear is a response to an unfamiliar stimulus and actually an inherited survival skill. Because fear is so emotionally overpowering, only physical reassurance from you will comfort your baby.

Responding to Your Baby's Interests

Besides reading your baby's signals accurately and responding to these signals promptly, you will need to learn to interact with your baby at her own level of interest and involvement; that is, you will learn to match your level of stimulation to your baby's behavior. For example, if your baby is happily splashing water, you will probably not be able to divert her attention to blowing bubbles, but you can show her as many alternate ways to splash water as you can. You are limited only by your own imagination.

New exercises can be briefly introduced, but then the old exercise can be resumed. In this manner, you can help your baby to make the transition from one activity to another smoothly, without making her apprehensive or inadvertently overstimulating her by pushing her into a water activity for which she is not yet ready.

Through such sensitive communication, baby learns that she can move and influence her environment without fear. Your baby will learn that you, as mom or dad, will be there when needed. With trusted parents near, stimulation from a new water experience can be securely dealt with, and that trust then develops into baby's own trust and confidence in her own water competence. The greater the degree of trust between you and your baby in the water, the greater her self-confidence and interest will be in exploring various water sensations and experiences.

Face-to-Face Interaction

The water experience provides a fascinating context for parent-baby communication. In some ways, baby's expressions may be easier for you to interpret while in the pool environment. For one thing, you have already decided to devote yourself to focusing on baby during his water time, and will probably be more receptive to his cues than you would ordinarily. And again, while in the water, you will be at eye level with one another for extended periods of time, which allows more face-to-face interaction (photo 4.10).

4.10. By sitting down in the water, you can place yourself at eye level with your baby.

By watching baby's face carefully at all times during the water adjustment phase, you can not only ensure that baby's mouth and nose remain above water, but also you can watch for "cues" that will enable you to judge how to proceed with any skill sequence. Should your baby show signs of being clingy or wary at any time during his water encounters, you need to rein in your own expectations and gear down in order to soothe your baby's fears and provide a firm foundation for future water experience.

5
Comfort Is Security

B abies must be physically comfortable to feel secure. Se-curity brings the freedom to explore, and discovery leads to learning. Learning is a process that requires a period of integration in dealing with external stimuli. If we are continuously "teaching" or "doing unto" baby, we distract baby from the very learning we are trying to encourage. Babies will go through several different learning experiences in water: *identification, exploration,* and *understanding.* Babies will first need to feel comfortable with the new sights and sounds and smells, and then they will learn to categorize and "use" these things. For example, if splashing water is too different from baby's prior experiences, or if the conditions surrounding the splashing are too active for baby, baby will become frustrated or over-stimulated and begin to cry. Each time a new experience or object is encountered, it becomes more familiar until baby is finally comfortable with it.

Babies will first need to get acquainted with the pool area itself. Bright light reflecting off the surface of the water can be an overwhelming sensory stimulus for your baby's developing nervous system. Bright lights will also intensify all other sensory information, so everything will seem to be louder and stronger. Swimming pools are large, open areas, and the vastness of the space itself can be an overwhelming encounter for a baby (photo 5.1). Chlorine vapors and moisture permeate the air. Locker room floors are cold and hard. Familiar clothes are removed and snug new swimsuits go on. After a period of time, this information will become familiar, your baby will learn the new pattern or routine, and the swimming pool and water environment will soon be a familiar, friendly place.

5.1. Unlike your home, pool areas are huge open spaces, full of bright lights and loud echoes that your baby will need time to adjust to.

Providing Friendly Sights, Sounds, and Feelings

Since you want to provide your baby with a nonthreatening environment, you can reduce the starkness of your baby's first encounter within the pool and locker room areas with soft lighting. By breaking the glare of light off the water's surface with colorful floating toys, we also extend an invitation to play and help to make the transition from bathtub to pool a happy one (photo 5.2).

5.2. Colorful toys are an invitation to play.

Babies can appreciate a full symphony orchestra, so why not have music in the pool? Choose music fitting to the water environment and your class activity. Flutes, harps, violins, and dulcimers shimmer and echo lightly through an enclosed area and set an uplifting and playful mood.

Music breaks the deep silence that surrounds water and cushions any loud or sudden noise. Bop music is overstimulating for babies in such a tactile environment as an enclosed swimming pool.

Babies have such tiny body masses that fifteen to twenty minutes in relatively warm water will turn little lips blue. Water temperature for babies' swimming classes should range from 86° to 94° F. Ideally, water temperature should remain within a five-degree range of the air temperature. Short dips in colder water are acceptable only if baby makes the decision to get in. Pull little ones out at the first sign of chilling or discomfort. Learning in the true sense of the word cannot take place if the child is cold, hungry, or frightened.

Thirty minutes is generally a standard class time period, because little ones learn best through short but frequent exposure to activity. Babies will probably not stay a full half hour for the first several water times (maybe only ten to fifteen minutes) and that's fine. Your baby's endurance levels to the excitement, activity, and water will increase as time goes by. As the excitement and interest in water play grow, your baby will also be willing to put up with a little discomfort and want to stay in longer, but the choice should always be your baby's.

Routine

Plan to give yourself a good half hour to forty-five minutes in the locker room before and after swimming, as babies need time to adapt to temperature changes comfortably.

To cut down on last-minute searches, you might want to keep a separate swim bag packed with the following:

1. A big fluffy towel (one for each wet body). Part of the pleasure of getting wet is the warmth and texture of the towel on cold, wet skin (photo 5.3).

5.3. A big fluffy towel for each wet body is a real baby-pleaser.

2. Shampoo to wash chlorine out of your and your baby's hair (conditioner, too).
3. Soft, cloth-lined plastic pants for babies who are not yet toilet trained.
4. A favorite water-proof toy.
5. Baby oil or lotion to restore moisture and proper pH of the skin and also for a brisk rubdown or massage.
6. Several plastic bags (from sandwich size to small trash bags) for wet suits and those wet surprises.
7. Juice, milk, and no-mess snacks.

Babies find much security in routine and if you swim at different places, or travel, pools can change, but babies (like adults) will find security within a routine. All water safety manuals recommend scouting out new swimming and diving areas before entering the water, so take baby in your arms or by the hand and explore together. Walk fully around the pool (photo 5.4) or walk the swimming area together looking for potential dangers such as soda tabs on an outdoor deck, or tree limbs on a river bank. Remove anything that could possibly cause harm. If that is impossible, move to another spot.

5.4. Because little ones don't often perceive what is at the other end of the pool, take your child's hand and explore the pool area together.

Once you have staked out a territory and laid down towels and assorted bags of clothes and equipment, you are ready to get into the water. Baby should sit in your lap or beside you on the pool deck (photo 5.5). If you are holding baby, be careful not to swing him out over the water as you seat yourself.

5.5. A baby too young to sit by himself can be seated in your lap, while an older one can sit beside you on the pool deck.

Water Entry

To enter the water from the deck, have someone else hold baby while you slip in. If you do not have a second pair of hands close by, scoot baby back away from the edge, ankles on the deck, so that baby cannot lunge forward as you slip in. Place one hand on baby's thigh (your closest hand on his closest thigh). Place your weight on the other hand that is resting on the deck, and slip slowly into the water. This takes a bit of practice to accomplish without splashing your baby. Move slowly, keeping an eye on baby.

Adjusting to Water Temperature

We have found that making this water entry practice routine before each swimming time encourages the babies to sit down

and wait for you to get wet first. Older children accept this
routine as part of their swimming and will sit and wait if mom
is lagging. The initial excitement of getting into the water also
seems to be a social event that babies enjoy sharing. So don't
hesitate to take the time for a slow and easy entry.

As you turn to face baby, you can begin to pull water up over
her feet to check her reaction to the water temperature. With
your baby's "OK," proceed to pull water up over knees and
thighs, watching baby's face closely for the "OK" before proceeding to the next stage (photo 5.6). With baby's "OK," pull
water slowly up over baby's tummy and chest (photo 5.7).
Watch for a surprised reaction or sudden intake of breath or
pulling away. This signals that baby is not ready to go on.

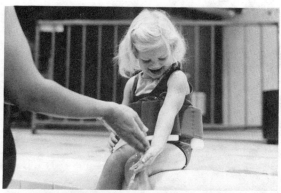

5.6. Pull water up over your baby's knees and thighs to help her adjust to the water temperature.

5.7. With your baby's "OK," you can pull water up over her tummy and chest.

Chest-to-Chest Close

When your baby is ready to follow you into the water, he will indicate his readiness by smiling, edging forward, and holding out his arms to you. Pull him gently to you (photo 5.8) and hold him chest-to-chest close (photo 5.9).

5.8. When your little one is ready to get in, pull her to you gently.

5.9. Relax together and take a few minutes to be physically close.

Wading In

You can follow the same adjustment sequence above for wading in, regardless of whether you are holding your baby chest-to-chest close or whether baby wades into the water beside you.

Once the water is happily pulled over your baby's tummy, you
can dip by bending your knees or you can walk to a water depth
that covers baby's shoulders (photo 5.10).

*5.10. Dip or walk to
a depth of water that
will cover your baby's
shoulders.*

Shoulders Under

Parents holding their babies chest-to-chest close in the water
should remain in relatively shallow water (photo 5.11). To adventure into deeper water will shift your center of gravity from
your pelvis to your chest. A sudden lunge by baby can cause
you both to take a dunking. It is better to remain in shallow
water, bending at the knees, until the water is at shoulder
level. If a problem arises, then all you need to do is stand up.

*5.11. Your balance is
more stable in shallow
water than in deep
water.*

Once your baby's shoulders are wet, keep them under water, because body heat will dissipate with moisture as it evaporates from the surface of the skin. Dressing baby in a three-quarter-length, sleeved T-shirt in the water will help to prevent chilling (photo 5.12). Be sure the T-shirt has been washed before. Swimming pool water contains chlorine, which is essentially bleach. Colorful new T-shirts tend to bleed wisps of color in the water and will stain other wet items thrown together in a bag. Babies who are still putting everything into their mouths will suck on sleeves that are too long, drinking any dye that bleeds from the material, so roll up long sleeves.

5.12. A long-sleeved T-shirt will help to prevent chilling.

Just as your baby needs to adjust to water temperature and changes in gravity and balance in water, you too will need time to feel comfortable, steady, and confident. Once both your shoulders and baby's are wet, you can walk around the pool, moving slowly and purposefully, looking at toys and numbered tiles and assorted goodies. Your baby will begin to reach and pull away from you when he is ready to explore. Until he gives you such indication, keep him chest-to-chest close.

Face-to-Face

After baby exhibits confidence by reaching away from you or trying to wriggle out of your arms, you can hold baby face-to-face with your hands encircling her rib cage (photo 5.13). Make special note of your thumbs. When adult thumbs rise above baby's collar bone, they can exert uncomfortable pressure on the soft fleshy areas of the neck, placing undue pressure on the esophagus and carotid arteries. Adult thumbs that rest on baby's shoulders can inhibit use of the arms.

5.13. Hold your little one with thumbs at nipple level.

Babies are slippery when wet. As your hands slip upward underneath baby's shoulders, you can walk them down baby again (photo 5.14). Should baby's hands turn blue, that means you are holding baby too tightly. It is a common reaction to hold baby tightly during your first few water encounters. Once you feel assured of your own water competence, your grip will relax naturally. Let the water support baby's body weight. Your hands are there only to keep baby upright. Check the position of your hands and thumbs on baby's body throughout your water time together.

5.14. You can walk your hands down baby's torso to readjust your hold.

6
Heads Up—
Bottoms Under

B abies and small children lying face down in the water cannot pull their heads through the surface tension of the water to take a breath. Since we all have some experience with not being able to breathe at will and with the feeling of panic that follows, we can empathize with baby and realize that the horizontal swimming position we all strive to achieve is uncomfortable for babies.

Using the Spine as a Lever

Your baby's spine acts as a lever to balance the weight of his head, and the longer the lever in this case, the more efficient control of his head your little one will have. Because body strength and spinal length are both lacking in infants and babies, the most comfortable position for them is vertical, heads upon shoulders, above pelvis and feet (photo 6.1).

6.1. Your child's first swimming position will be a standing one.

Babies are natural "floaters," and your baby's bottom will naturally float to the surface. You can help your baby to simulate the vertical position by gently pushing his feet and bottom under. As your baby's bottom floats to the surface, his feet will follow, and unexercised bodies have to work overtime to keep the face from plopping forward into the water (photo 6.2).

6.2. Most parents initially try to hold their children horizontally on top of the water, but should your baby's hips or feet break the water surface you can expect a dunking.

The vertical position must be maintained as we progress through the skill sequencing or baby's face will continue to plunk into the water. Rest assured that as your baby's body strength and spinal length increase during the normal course of development, his body position will naturally angle out until he is completely horizontal in the water. (The general age for a child's body to reach the length and strength to pull the head from the water and stroke above water in a semi-horizontal or horizontal position will be around three to five (photo 6.3).

6.3. Only after your baby is long and strong enough to lift his head and arms from the water, when he is between the ages of 3 and 5, will he swim horizontally. Most early horizontal swimming will be underwater.

Until that time, the vertical position is what we will concentrate on helping your baby achieve. All skill sequences of the Water Play program are designed for use with this position.

Licking Water

Now that your baby has the "feel" for heads up—bottoms under, you will want to begin to help her identify water. She has splashed in it, kicked it, found it in her eyes and ears, but the real identification occurs as she tastes water.

Hold your baby face-to-face and immersed in water to her

shoulders, making sure her bottom is under (photo 6.4). Make all the smacking and eating sounds you can. Even tiny babies are captivated by these sounds and will imitate your actions. While the water in the pool is calm, you can gently lower your baby's chin (be sure her bottom doesn't float to the surface) into the water so that a wave will gently wash over her bottom lip (photo 6.5).

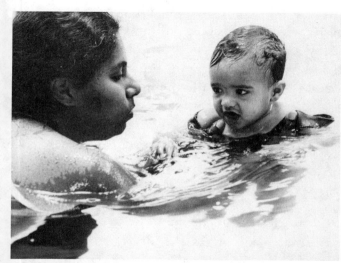

6.4. *Most parents tend to tip baby forward to meet face-to-face. Make sure baby is in a standing position and that his bottom doesn't float to the surface while your attention is directed toward baby's face and you are licking the water.*

6.5. *Allow a ripple of water to wash over baby's bottom lip.*

Babies need to identify water by licking it and to experiment with water to see what can be done with it. While licking, your baby will swallow only drinkable amounts of water. (You will find this to be true as you practice your own licking, bubbles, and whale spouts.) Muscles of swallowing and respiration are strengthened by this exercise and are obviously the most important aspect of control and confidence that you can offer your baby in water.

Performed correctly, three to five minutes of licking exercises cannot cause water intoxication. Reported cases of hyponatremia have occurred only with forced immersions: pulling baby under water, or pushing baby under water and then through the water. Tasting and licking water should never become a forced immersion because we are not training the diving reflex.

Bubbles

Bubbles are just additional exercises in licking. Air is exhaled under the surface of the water so that as the air rises to the surface, bubbles are made (photo 6.6). Exhaling under the surface of the water is a difficult task for most babies. It takes

6.6. *Exhaling under the water creates bubbles, which tickle baby's cheeks.*

considerable muscular control of the diaphragm and upper respiratory system to push air out of the nostrils and mouth into the water, breaking the water pressure around the mouth.

All babies love to hum and gurgle. Throat noises of any kind are terrific fun, and a myriad of verbal exchanges can be enhanced by making them underwater. Try singing "Old McDonald" or "Happy Birthday" to your baby underwater. Older children love to put an ear under to listen to the song and can often tell you which song you are singing.

Coughing and Sputters

Your baby's bottom will often float to the surface of the water while you are concentrating on the licking and bubbles, causing your baby's face to suddenly plunk into the water and surprising everyone. (As this will usually occur more than once in your baby's swimming life, you will have plenty of opportunity to learn to slow and calm your own movements.) Most parents automatically react to this by abruptly standing up and jerking baby out of the water.

So as not to add to your baby's alarm, keep your own movements slow and rhythmic. Touch your baby first, then close your hands around him. As you pull him from the water, pull him up head first, so that water is not forced into his nostrils and sinuses (photo 6.7). Once your baby has been righted, you can hold one of his arms straight up, high above the head and close to the ear. This will stretch muscles upward around the rib cage and diaphragm, helping to ease the coughing spasm (photo 6.8). This constructive action also prevents you from patting baby on the back, which increases baby's disorientation and makes coughing up water more laborious. Older babies helped in this manner automatically hold up their own arms after taking a dunking.

6.7. *Lift your baby from the water headfirst after a dunking to prevent water from being forced into the nostrils.*

6.8. *Lifting an arm above the head stretches the muscles that are contracting during the coughing and helps to ease the sputters.*

Imitating baby's coughing sounds is also very reassuring for your little one and is often turned into a game. Be sensitive, though, to the reality of the trauma, and imitate the coughing or use laughter only when you sense there is no fear or sudden surprise involved in the dunking. Smile, even though your heart may be in your stomach, and talk to baby throughout the coughing. Be honest with any words of praise and comfort. "My, did you surprise Mommy, but you handled that so well!" is a positive exclamation. It recognizes the suddenness and shock, but at the same time acknowledges your baby's personal power in dealing effectively with the threat. After several hugs, your baby will begin to show renewed interest in his water play and you can then introduce a new toy or draw attention to someone else to help minimize his discomfort.

Facial Flushes

Wet faces will sometimes flush red above the eyebrows and below the eyes across the cheeks. This means that baby has snorted water into the nostrils and up into the sinuses. As you know, this stings like crazy. Your baby will be quite unhappy with this experience (sometimes climbing you like a monkey climbing a tree) and will loudly vocalize her protests. Hold your baby close and comfort her until the pressures equalize and the water drains from the sinuses.

You will notice in watching your baby's face that, after such an episode, she does a lot of swallowing and makes eating motions with her mouth. This is because water is draining from the sinuses down the back of the throat. Applying soft fingertip pressure above the brows and along the cheek bones beneath the eyes will sometimes help. If baby protests, it is better just to let the water drain naturally.

Whale Spouts

Whale spouts are really just sophisticated spitting. Water is drawn into the mouth and spit out again (photo 6.9). This is the one water task that parents have the most difficulty learning. Whale spouts look so simple and easy to perform, but they take concentration, and muscles need practice in order to strengthen control of the arch of the spout. Whale spouts offer parents first-hand experience in the difficulty babies have in blowing bubbles or in swallowing and spitting out water. Parents can experience their own changing competence levels with whale spouts through practice and, from personal experience, are better able to "see" and empathize with baby's progress in the water.

6.9. Whale spouts delight babies and parents alike.

Fussy Babies

If at any time during these exercises your baby becomes fussy, check for goose bumps and blueing lips, which would indicate he is cold. If your baby is not cold, it is possible that he is hungry. Bring a bottle or find a quiet spot in the water where you can nurse baby (photo 6.10), or climb out and take a short snack break.

6.10. Water activity builds an appetite, so quiet snack breaks are important.

Eating before swimming does not cause stomach cramps but you'll want your baby to avoid swimming on a full stomach to avoid "burp ups." In general, you can feed older babies protein foods a good hour before swimming. Babies on milk should be fed no later than one hour before class. Snacks during class are often a source of comfort as well as a means of appeasing hunger pangs. This is fine, but it is advisable to discontinue water licking and bubble or spout exercises for that class.

If your baby does not appear cold and will not take food but still acts fussy, you can mentally scan the last few days as you get dressed. Has the baby's day-to-day schedule been interrupted by house guests or workers? Did he miss his morning nap? Is he running a slight temperature with teething or a cold? (The temperature or the tactile stimulation of feverish skin can actually hurt.) Just as with adults, there will be days when the last thing in the world your baby will want to do is to get wet.

Getting Out

Older babies, even those not yet speaking, can communicate that they are ready to get out of the pool and dry off. Most do so by climbing out and acting reluctant to get back in (photo 6.11). A few enterprising little ones understand that a towel brings a water class to an end (photo 6.12).

6.11. Children not yet speaking can communicate their readiness to get dry by climbing out and acting reluctant to get back into the water.

6.12. *Handing mom a towel is a sure sign that this child is ready to dry off.*

7
Buoyancy First

A ll babies are naturally buoyant due to large amounts of adipose tissue. Your hands can actually feel how buoyant your baby is in the water, helping you to estimate just how much support you'll need to offer. With your hands helping baby to maintain the vertical position, baby is free to discover the balance necessary to maintain her position. Your baby now needs to develop the respiratory skills necessary to maintain a comfortable degree of buoyancy.

As your baby's own body growth is perpetually changing, her center of gravity and balance are also continually changing. In the water, your baby's center of gravity will shift from the pelvis to the chest (photo 7.1). Because your baby is so short and her lungs are small, her center of gravity is more accurately estimated high on the chest cavity near the shoulders. This means that your baby must remain shoulder deep in water for optimum balance (photo 7.2).

7.1. *In the water, your baby's center of gravity shifts from the hips to the upper torso.*

7.2. *Your baby will feel most secure in a standing position in shoulder-depth water. (Photo by Michael Kadner)*

Bobbing

Each time your baby takes a breath, the volume of air in her lungs increases, causing her body to rise in the water. Steady breathing in and out causes a mild bobbing action, but a sharp inhaling will cause your baby to rise suddenly and a sudden exhalation to drop just as suddenly.

When shoulders are underneath the water surface, the water level will be very near the mouth, if not covering it. And because babies have difficulty controlling the weight of their heads, this is a prime position for snorting and drinking water, even during gentle bobbing. Because water encounters are full of surprises (and swimming is an aerobic exercise), your baby will need a little extra buoyancy until she develops the respiratory strength to regulate better her breathing.

"Tubie Suits"

For these reasons, the Water Play program supports the use of "tubie suits," which are a flotation aid. Tubie suits are unisex tank suits with oblong pockets stitched around the back and chest. Tubes of styrofoam or polyethylene fit into the pockets and are removed one at a time as your baby gains in body strength and buoyancy. Tubie suits lower the center of gravity from the shoulder area of the chest toward the diaphragm area of the chest cavity, giving your baby extra buoyancy (and you a little more courage) in experimenting with buoyancy and balance (photo 7.3).

7.3. *When used correctly, tubie suits provide the additional buoyancy necessary for children to develop their own respiratory strength and control.*

Water will offer babies in tubie suits extended opportunities to discover and rediscover the most efficient level of buoyancy necessary for balance. The rocking motion of the water offers its own gentle challenge to maintaining a steady buoyant pattern. Each current of water will change your baby's balance and elicit a counter movement from him in order to maintain his balance. Your baby's buoyancy and balance require total body awareness, which involves a sense of left-right, front-back and top-bottom.

By extending his arms, and by pushing down onto your hands or arms in the water, your baby can experiment with buoyancy and balance (photo 7.4). The heads-up-bottoms-under position that you have been so careful to support and encourage with baby in the water will now begin to make sense. As baby has become proficient in water-adjustment skills and confident in his water experience, he will begin to lean away from you and to reach away from you in the water. Following your baby's "cues," you can increase the distance between you and baby without yet withdrawing your physical support.

7.4. By pushing down on your hands, your baby can experiment with bobbing up and down.

Two-Hand Hold

Holding both of baby's hands in yours (photo 7.5), try only to support baby's body weight aided by the tubie suit. Your hands should support only baby's vertical balance, keeping baby upright. Your baby's body weight should be entirely supported by the water. If baby's shoulders are completely out of the water, then you are lifting her upward with your hands, or there may be one too many tubes inserted in the suit. Relax and gently lower your own shoulders and hands under the water (or remove one tube from the center in back) until you feel the water supporting baby's body weight (photo 7.6). Baby gets more exercise the less you help, and unused muscles will strengthen more quickly.

7.5. Should your baby's shoulders rise above the water, you are lifting baby up.

7.6. As your baby pushes down on your palms, lower your hands beneath the water's surface until your baby's shoulders are underwater.

Beginning Dance Steps

While you are holding baby face-to-face, walk slowly backward in the water, pulling baby with you. He can use the muscles in the arms, shoulders, neck, and back to maintain his balance in the changing currents. When you begin to walk backward, the resistance of the water and the natural buoyancy of your baby's bottom will push his legs out behind his torso so the bottom will bob to the surface (photo 7.7). Your baby will respond to the change of body position by resting his weight on his hands. Your hands will probably feel his weight shift before you see him change position.

7.7. Holding your little one's hands, walk backward in the water, and watch her hips and legs surface.

By walking forward in the water, the same principles apply, but in reverse. Little legs will be pushed down, bottoms will go under, and baby's feet will angle in toward you (photo 7.8). If you move too quickly or raise your hands up out of the water while walking forward, baby will end up in an awkward back float position. So relax and move slowly and rhythmically.

7.8. When you walk forward in the water, your baby's legs will extend toward you as she inclines.

Try walking forward and then backward until you feel a rhythm between you and your baby. Babies love the sensation of buoyancy and are delighted with the sensations that occur with a change of direction. You should be able to anticipate your baby's bodily response to each movement you make in the water. And baby will, from your movements and the changing water currents, begin to adapt to the most efficient movement patterns for keeping his head above water. As you become comfortable with water dancing, these same "steps" can be accomplished with just a turning of your wrists.

Draping

By "draping" your baby over the crook of your outstretched left arm and supporting baby with your free hand. By drawing baby in a wide circle, you can offer her variations in body position that will allow her more control and opportunity for developing body strength (photo 7.9). As you feel comfortable with the exercise, you can change direction and then switch to your right arm (photo 7.10). Notice the change in the position of your baby's feet and what that change means in relationship to the position of baby's head.

7.9. *"Drape" baby over your left forearm and pull him in a wide circle.*

7.10. Now switch to your right forearm.

Sitting

Shift back to your palms-up position. As your hands feel that your baby is balanced, you can walk one hand, then the other down to grasp baby's hips, making a seat for your baby (photo 7.11). You may have to lean forward in the water, holding baby in your extended arms. As your balance and baby's balance harmonize, you can walk one hand down to grasp baby's leg just above the back of the knee (photo 7.12). Watch for baby's reaction and make sure his balance and your own are steady before proceeding to move your hand to the back of his other knee. As your movements become rhythmic and steady (this may actually take several classes), you can then walk one hand down to grasp baby's ankle (photo 7.13). Baby must straighten that first leg in your grasp at the knee before you try to hold the other ankle or he will lose his balance.

7.11. Make a seat for your child with your hands.

7.12. Then walk one hand down to grasp the back of his knee.

7.13. Shift your other hand to grasp the other knee, so that you are now holding your baby evenly balanced.

Standing

Even small babies can stand upright in the water. If baby won't extend the leg at the knee, place your palms underneath baby's feet instead of holding at the ankle. The pressure of your palm on the ball of baby's foot will usually prompt baby to meet that pressure by stepping down or pressing her foot against your palm. Place one hand at a time underneath a foot (photo 7.14), moving deliberately and smoothly. When baby is firmly standing in your palms you will need to respond by "dancing" in large, wide movements. Depending upon the length of your arms and baby's height, you may have to really stretch forward and do some fancy footwork to keep baby balanced.

7.14. Let your child stand in your palms. Be sure to keep his feet underneath his hips.

Retrieving Baby

With all this activity, your baby is most likely to take a dunking or two. Adult hands should always close lightly and smoothly around little bodies, to avoid startling them underwater. Retrieval from the water should always be head first so that baby's head is not forced to drop back in, breaking the surface tension of the water and forcing water into nostrils and sinuses. Retrievals can be made by grasping an arm or shoulder and pulling up and out of the water (photo 7.15). If baby has taken in a mouthful of water and sputters, her arm should be raised above her head and she should be held closely and comforted. Either way when water work is resumed, it should begin at a slower pace, gradually working back to the activity level that you left.

7.15. Should your baby lose her balance, step forward and pull her up to you at the same time. You can also bring a knee up to help lift her from the water.

Back Float Preparation

For obvious reasons, back floats should be practiced only in calm water. If in doubt as to whether the water is calm enough, wait. If your baby is in a pool with older, more active children, you might want to forgo back floats altogether.

Even warm water will feel cool to the outer and middle ears and babies will often resist back floats because of this temperature difference. So, as with the initial water adjustment sequence, we need to help baby prepare for back floats. You will first need to pull water in stages up over the back of your baby's shoulders, neck, and head. Watch for baby's reaction and "OK" before proceeding from one stage to the next.

Baby's Back Float Body Position

Like the vertical position, back floats will be more comfortable and less threatening to baby if the weight of his head is always supported higher than his hips and feet. Instead of a completely horizontal position, we want baby on an upward-sloping angle. Envision a staircase, with baby's head at the top and feet at the bottom (photo 7.16). Bottoms will still tend to float to the surface, but unlike the vertical position, you will not be able to push tummies underwater on a back float because baby will bend at the waist. If you move a hand down to the thighs, however, just above the knee, and push down gently, bottoms will submerge.

7.16. Back floats should begin with the ears above water.

As you walk backward, drawing your baby headfirst through the water, you can rest his head upon your shoulder or your chest.

As baby becomes familiar with the back float sensations, he will relax and stretch out in the water (photo 7.17). His head will drop back comfortably into the water, getting the ears wet. Your hands will be able to feel him relax. At this time you can begin to support your baby by holding his head in your hands (photo 7.18), ideally with fingertips resting upon his cheek and jaw. Remember to keep moving baby through the water head-first. Relax your hands until you can feel that your baby's weight is supported by the water. Fingertips should remain at baby's temples until baby can balance by himself.

7.17. As babies relax and begin to enjoy back floats, they naturally stretch out in the water.

7.18. Place your hands underneath baby's shoulders and neck.

Learning to maintain the balance on the back is fairly much determined by the amount of opportunity parental hands offer. Some babies will be so relaxed with floating that they can fall asleep and float unaided (but always closely attended).

Back Float Retrievals

Should water wash over baby's face during a floating sequence, lift baby's head first from the water, so that water is not forced into the nostrils and sinuses. Keep baby vertical and chest-to-chest close, lifting her arm into the air, talking to and soothing her until she is settled (photo 7.19). Look for facial flushes and swallowing motions and give baby plenty of recovery time before resuming the back floats.

Because babies, especially those who are just learning to sit and stand, value their new postural prowess, they will often oppose back floats until some time after walking and then "rediscover" back float sensations that they will perform endlessly on their own.

7.19. Retrievals from a back float should always be made by lifting baby headfirst from the water.

The best approach is just to *offer* your baby adequate support for floating and let her decide what sensations she wants to experience.

8
Balance Is Independence

B uoyancy and balance are much entwined. Without first ex-
periencing the sensation of buoyancy and without first
adjusting to the altered center of gravity, swimming skills cannot develop. Older children and adults who are fearful of water
and cannot learn to swim, no matter how persistent they are,
need to spend more time practicing buoyancy and balance
skills. As these skills are mastered, self-confidence and pleasure
increase and the fear is forgotten.

What your child learns now about buoyancy and balance will
affect his attitude toward water and swimming throughout his
life.

Should these learning stages be rushed, as they are in most
age-group swimming classes, your child may never feel comfortable in the water environment even though she does learn to
swim.

A Personal Experience

Buoyancy and balance are personal experiences that are different
for everyone. Each baby needs a different amount of time to

become familiar with the sensations of buoyancy. She will need time to relax and explore how her various movements change these sensations and her balance. Only after your baby has a strong background of water experiences will she feel confident enough to experiment and implement change.

The exercises in Chapter 7 will have helped both you and your baby to experience sensations of buoyancy and balance as well as changes in movement and direction. As your baby's control strengthens and the water sensations become familiar, your baby will become more self-confident and will begin to initiate new water movements.

Weaning

For many new parents, water weaning causes some emotional turmoil, just as does weaning baby from the breast or the bottle. The close physical dependency that your baby has shared with you in the water is changing, and it is reassuring to you to try to hold onto it a little bit longer.

But "holding on" to your little one will limit his water progress. So you will want to prepare for this time by turning your attention to the physical details of your water interaction.

Throughout the hands-on maneuvers, you were holding your little one with both hands. Now you can begin to practice the same exercises with open palms.

Palms Up

Place your hands palms upward, just underneath the surface of the water. Baby can grasp your hands by placing his own hands in your open palms (photo 8.1). As you practice the different exercises you may want to offer baby a little extra support during turns and sudden movements. But be aware of your hands at all times. Your palms can "feel" when your support is really needed.

8.1. Baby can grasp your hands by placing hers in your open palms.

Two-Hand Hold

This is still a two-hand hold, but it is your baby who should now be supporting her own body position by holding onto you with both hands. Remember, if baby's shoulders and chest are above the surface of the water, you are lifting her upward. Relax your own shoulders and release the tension that you feel running through your forearms.

In your palms-up position, repeat your forward and backward water dance steps (photos 8.2 and 8.3), then with baby's "OK" go onto the draping exercises (photo 8.4). Let baby hold on by herself, and try not to give any additional support with your hands (photo 8.5).

8.2. *Left: With arms extended, walk forward in the water.*

8.3. *Middle: With fluid movements, reverse your direction and walk backward, watching the effect your movement has had upon your baby's position in the water.*

8.4. *Below left: Let baby hold onto your extended arm as you draw her in a wide circle.*

8.5. *Below right: Begin to really relax and let your baby hang onto you. Continue to offer an arm, leg, or your torso for support, but let him do the balancing work.*

Wall Work

Two-hand holds can also be performed at the wall of the pool (older pools have gutter lines, newer pools have hand holds). Older babies can stand; younger babies can be assisted. By assuming a sitting position in the water, you can give baby a thigh base on which to sit or stand. Allow baby to hold at the wall with both hands (photo 8.6). Babies love to bounce by placing their feet on the wall and jumping.

8.6. Let your child hold onto the wall of the pool by herself. Position a knee underneath her for support, if desired.

Keep a watchful eye. Younger babies tend to sit down suddenly or release their hold on the wall. Older babies, realizing that for the first time they are actually independent of your support (we won't count your knees because wading pools have shallow water where babies can stand), often want to push forcefully away from the wall.

Dunkings

Dunkings take on a new dimension in light of this newly found independence. Although more frequent during this stage of your baby's water development, dunkings become less of an issue. Be sensitive to your baby's needs. Toward the end of a swimming period, babies will be tired and dunkings will become more frequent. During any one water time, two or three good dunkings are enough frustration for anyone. Rather than tire your baby out or set him back several paces in self-confidence, move in and offer more physical support toward the end of a class or on an "off" day. To help your baby remain as independent as possible, you can add another tubie or two.

Balance Is Independence

After several classes with two-hand holds, using a stable support like the wall, you can ease baby into two-hand holds with a floating support such as a kickboard (photo 8.7) or an unstable support such as the lane line (photo 8.8). Initially, baby may need some assistance, so stay close. Your baby will, after some practice, be completely independent and will know it. The look is one of wonder, excitement, and disbelief.

8.7

8.8. Floating supports such as kickboards or the lane line are more difficult to balance on. (Photo by Michael Kadner)

Most babies are capable of this buoyancy with flotation support before they can walk.

Flippers

Babies should use flippers during these independent floating sessions to aid their stability and balance (photo 8.9). Longer flippers are better for shorter or younger babies. The smaller flippers are better suited to taller or older babies who do not need additional body length for support.

Babies wearing flippers in shallow water seem to sense the pool bottom and the additional length of the flipper. They tend to draw their knees upward. Take baby into deeper water and he will straighten out again.

8.9. Flippers will slow your baby's movements, giving you both extra recovery time.

One-Hand Holds

A two-hand hold in water is equivalent to your baby's standing on land. One-hand holds will develop naturally from the two-hand holds. This changeover is equivalent to your baby's first step on land and cause for much excitement in the pool (photo 8.10).

Walking with all fours around the gutter line or edge of the pool becomes a great challenge, and independence from one-hand holds on floating supports and unstable supports can be encouraged by placing brightly colored floating toys just within your baby's reach (photo 8.11).

8.10. One-hand holds develop naturally from two-hand holds.

8.11 Place toys within reach to encourage your child to develop greater independence.

Encircling

By extending both arms in a loose circle in front of you and placing your baby between them, she can balance herself. By walking forward and backward in the water you can help keep baby vertical. If baby's shoulders break above the surface of the water, your arms are lifting her upward. When her shoulders and chest come out of the water, she loses the necessary length underneath the water for balance and stability. When your baby's shoulders remain close to the water surface, the water will act to brace her and can offer her greater stability.

Lightly encircle baby with your arms. Don't use your hands, but let her balance, using you to climb on and hold onto (photo 8.12).

8.12. Encircle baby lightly with your arms.

Spread your arms wider and let baby balance momentarily alone (photo 8.13). While baby is learning to balance, both feet will often float up behind. Flippers will slow the movement time (photo 8.9), giving her a chance to recover her balance on her own.

8.13. Widen circle around baby slowly and deliberately spread your arms apart, allowing him to balance momentarily alone.

At this stage of independence, your assistance will drop off to a few reassuring hugs and a helpful hand to push a wayward foot under (photo 8.14).

8.14. At this stage of independence, your assistance will drop off to a few reassuring hugs and a helpful hand to push a stray foot under.

Floating Toys

Floating toys, because they contain air, will also provide transitional support from the kickboard or lane line. It is not uncommon to see a pool full of babies with a floating toy in each hand. Parents often complain that they want their babies to pay more attention to swimming and play less with the toys, but these little guys are using the toys as a flotation aid and to help them balance. Remember what it was like to push a small beach ball underneath you in the water?

Later, when your baby discovers "speed" of movement, the toys will slow him down and he will direct his attention more and more toward refining his forward movement in the water, and drop the toys altogether.

Circles

Your baby's first independent directional movement in the water will probably be a circular movement. The head turns to look for you or to follow a toy and the body follows the turn of the head (photo 8.15).

8.15. Where your little one looks with the eyes and head is the direction in which she will move.

Log Rolling

As circles are performed faster, babies often lose their balance. As the feet rise toward the surface, the head plops forward. In this near horizontal position, circles become a full body twist that the older babies named "log rolling" (photo 8.16). The tubie suit will keep baby on the surface of the water, but you will have to step in and stop the roll and help your baby regain her balance. After a bit of experience your baby will be able to prevent herself from beginning a "log roll" by turning her head upward to look at the lights in the ceiling above. We first explain to the older babies that if their mouths get wet all they need to do is look up at the lights in the ceiling. Later all you will need to say to remind your little one is "look up" (photo 8.17).

8.16. Left: *Rolling rapidly in the water is great fun, but it takes some effort to stop the roll.*
8.17. Above: *Your baby can be "cued" to look up at the lights in the ceiling to pull out of the roll.*

Push Offs

Push offs begin as a two-hand hold at the wall. You will demonstrate the first one by saying "look up" and then "put your head back in the water." Together, you can then count, "one, two, three, *push* off" (photo 8.18). You can stand behind baby and assist her first few push offs so that she doesn't take a dunking. Pulling out of the short back glide after the push off often becomes a log roll, so stay close.

8.18. *Push offs begin at the wall with a two-hand hold. Tell your child to put her head back in the water and push off from the wall with her feet.*

Catch

Toys are also fun to play catch with. Throwing a toy in water is different from throwing a toy on land because in the water you have no solid support underneath you. So, as the baby lifts the arm above the head, the weight of the arm and the toy will bob your baby downward (photo 8.19). As baby releases the toy in surprise and drops his arm, the bobbing gets stronger and it will take a few breaths to smooth things out. Playing with toys in the water will enable your little one to understand a variety of subtleties in water movement. So by all means encourage the use of water toys (photo 8.20).

8.19. Lifting the arm to throw will cause your baby to bob in the water.

8.20. Encourage your child to reach and throw with the use of brightly colored toys.

9
Self-Confident Independence Leads to Swimming

W ithout confidence in his ability to deal effectively with water in the eyes, ears, and mouth, your child will approach new water experiences with some caution. Caution inhibits baby's movement. So, what you will want to look for in any stage of water learning is confident movement. That means your baby will fully extend his arms and legs in the water and actively move about. Should your child keep his arms and legs close to the torso while moving or try to move closer to you in the water, you both need a bit more time to work on balance skills together before proceeding to the swimming skills outlined in this chapter.

Beginning Swimming Skills

Forward movement in water begins for the younger babies in a frog-like thrust of the torso (photo 9.1) that modifies over time into a bicycle kick. Most babies will bring the knees almost to the surface (photo 9.2). Later, the flexion of the knee will lessen and the ankles will extend more and a flutter kick of sorts will develop (photo 9.3).

As the kicking pattern gradually changes, your baby's body position in the water will begin to angle forward, away from the vertical position. Baby's hands will begin to press downward on the water to balance and to right the inclining head (photo 9.4). The stroking pattern then develops. Some babies swish their hands lightly in the water and others prefer to thrash their way forward, drenching all.

9.1. For infants, forward movement in the water begins with a reflexive frog kick.

9.2. Later, the frog kick will develop into a bicycle kick.

9.3. Still later, the bicycle kick will develop into a flutter kick.

9.4. Only after your child's body begins to angle forward in the water will she begin to press down on the water for balance. It is from the need for balance that stroking with the arms develops.

This forward movement involves rhythm and synchronization of body movement. Rhythm and coordination of body movement reflect your child's understanding of time. As movement causes the body to progress through the water, a succession of points in the pool can be explored. These points can then be revisited quickly or slowly. Through the experience of controlling the tempo of body movement in the water, your baby will develop her own sense of distance and duration.

Toys or helping adults can also be strategically placed to encourage the direction and the distance to be covered by your baby. As the distance increases, the baby's kicking pattern will selectively smooth out.

Individual Swimming Styles

It does not matter what your baby's kicking and stroking patterns look like because they are going to be changing all the time. New patterns are continually explored, and baby's own nervous system will choose the pattern that is most efficient for the particular movement desired. At this time, self-discovery and exploration should take precedence.

Adult lap-swimmers and swimming competitors are disciplined and directed in their swimming strokes, but babies needing to explore are happiest and most comfortable just forging along, stopping to look here, making up with a burst of intensive movement, only to be interrupted by a brightly colored toy in someone else's possession (photo 9.5).

9.5. Children are happiest and most comfortable just foraging along in the water.

Reducing Buoyancy

As your little one develops forward movement in water and his body angle changes, you can symmetrically remove one or two tubies at a time to keep his chin level in the water (photo 9.6). You can even cut tubies in half or in quarters if removing one tubie is too much of a reduction.

9.6. *You can remove tubies one or two at a time to keep your baby's chin level in the water.*

There will come a time when the tubies actually hinder movement rather than aid it, and your child will ask to take the suit off or just refuse to wear it any longer.

Continue to reduce your child's buoyancy until all the tubies have been removed.

The First Swim Without Tubies

Without the tubie suit, your baby's early body position will be vertical, with the back of the head in the water (photo 9.7). Her chest will begin to break the surface of the water as breath control strengthens, pulling the feet upward and nearer the surface of the water. Because your baby is looking backward, the first independent swimming will be a backstroke of sorts because any kicking or pulling will lift the hips and propel her backward in the water. By dropping the chin toward the chest and looking straight up, your baby can resume a resting position. Encourage your baby to stroke and kick underneath the water's surface so water isn't splashed in her face. Turning over in the water will follow naturally and short spurts of a dog paddle will gradually grow longer between resting in a back float and spurts of swimming backward. Dog paddle strokes should also be performed underneath the water surface for the same reasons.

9.7. Your child's body position without tubies will be vertical, with the head back in the water.

The crawl and the backstroking patterns, as we know them, with arms returning out of the water, will develop after your child's body position becomes more horizontal in the water. Just as in the tubie suit, lifting the arm from the water will also alter your baby's buoyancy, pushing her down into the water.

Front Floats

Front floats will not be comfortable for your child until he can dog paddle and turn over on his back to rest with ease. Front floats will increase in length naturally as your child's breath control increases. When the front float is mastered, a front push-off can be demonstrated at the wall. Begin with the two-hand hold, your baby's back to the wall (photo 9.8). Together count, "one, two, three, push off!" You can help your child increase the glide distance by counting for him while his face is in the water or by increasing the distance you stand from the wall so that he has farther to swim to you.

9.8. Begin with a two-hand hold on the deck, with the child's back to the wall.

Jumping

Your child can begin by sitting on the deck and scooting forward into your waiting arms (photo 9.9). As she becomes increasingly bold you can try a standing jump from the deck (photo 9.10). Most babies this independent love to fling themselves into the water again and again. Initially they should be caught in the water from a jump, keeping their heads well above water. Adding a swirl to the catch is a natural motion and a lot of fun (photo 9.11). Later, you yourself can go under water to catch your child (photos 9.12 and 9.13).

9.9. Jumping begins with staying close to the deck and to you.

9.10. *As your child's confidence grows, he will need less contact for security.*

9.11. *After the catch in midair, this mother swirls her child around in the water.*

9.12. *Nicholas is an old-timer at jumping, so now his mother waits for him underneath the water.*

9.13

9.14

Sitting Dive

Standing in front of your child, have her sit on the deck and hold her hands together over her head so that her upper arms cover her ears and so that her elbows and are straight. The soles of her feet should be in a "push" position on the pool wall. Next have her lean forward from the waist, tucking in the chin and lowering the hands toward the water's surface. Count together, "one, two, three, dive." On "dive," coach your little one to push off with her feet. At the same time, pull her hands down and into position for a shallow (not a deep) dive. Step to the side, and, as your child enters the water, you can release her hands.

Standing Dive

Children who swim independently without a swimming aid can venture with mom and dad into deep water. Watch other people dive first, so that your little one can see how it's done. You can explain what he's watching and answer any questions he might have. You'll need two adults to assist in a standing dive—one to help with the child's body positioning and to generally "spot" the dive, and the other to remain in the water to assist the child in surfacing.

Have the child stand with toes curled over the edge of the pool. Standing to one side of the child, help position his arms above his head so that upper arms cover the ears and elbows and are straight. Make sure the chin is tucked in toward the chest. Talk to the child to explain what you are doing so that he won't be surprised by any sudden movement or touch.

Have your little one lean forward at the waist, keeping the knees straight and dropping the hands below the knees. On the count of three, he can slowly lean into the dive. The adult in the pool can provide encouragement and assistance if needed.

Often times children don't straighten out their bodies when they enter the water from a dive, and the water will then push the bent body under and toward the edge of the pool, causing the child to turn a somersault in the water. Somersaults, as well as the jolt of hitting the water, can be disorienting, so it's imperative that a swimming adult be in the water. You can use a kickboard for support so you don't tire.

As the little one gains confidence with diving, he'll want to do it all by himself and will naturally begin to bend the knees and push off with the feet during the dive. All dives should be kept near the surface.

Growing Self-Confidence

You will find that as your child begins to float independently and then to direct his water movements, the distance between the two of you will increase and your child will begin to interact with other parents and children in the water.

Initially, your baby will choose to stay close to you in the water. But as his water skills and confidence increase, he will test out this new independence by swimming further away from you, looking back, and then moving even further away. Getting too far away, or a sudden noise or activity in the pool area will usually send him scurrying back to you. After a brief exchange, he will be off again.

On land, babies will eventually feel confident enough to venture into another room where you can't be seen. In the water, however, you don't want to become overly certain of your baby's confidence. Any sudden movement can send him into a log roll, so you'll want to follow him in the water, keeping just close enough to comfortably help in any retrieval.

Sociable Babies

Babies who can move independently in the water do not have to concentrate so hard on maintaining their balance and therefore become quite sociable. Swimming over to visit a buddy becomes a new game! This new water skill also encourages more land contact among the children.

Anna Rachel would greet each class with a sunny "Good morning" to all as she and her daddy, Nat, entered the pool area.

After swimming, snacks became a sharing event that all the babies looked forward to. Hayley and her mother, Francine, brought a box of strawberries to every swimming class. And it was Hayley's cheerful responsibility to give each child a "grawberry."

10
Underwater Play

U nderwater play is based upon principles of trust and enjoyment between you and your baby. It is also based upon a
series of successful and happy interactions—yours as well as
your baby's—with the water. You, too, have to develop a "feel"
for the water and rhythm in moving with your baby in the
water. If your body movements are not yet harmonious with
your baby's above water, being able to respond to your baby's
needs beneath the water, where sight and sound are distorted,
will be almost impossible.

If you are hesitant or baby is unhappy about getting his face
wet, you need more time to happily encounter water together
and time to share those successful happy experiences.

Babies who are not adept and happy with licking, bubbles,
and whale spouts, and babies who are still upset by coughing
should wait until they can perform these skills happily and
comfortably. Waiting recognizes baby's personal need to be in
control of his own actions and the environment. We have all
been placed in a situation where we felt we had very little control. If that situation also includes a threat to our very lives, as

in an accident or natural disaster, the experience can be devastating. Not being able to breathe underwater when you need to can cause that same kind of overwhelming fear and panic.

Underwater play, although play, is serious business. Physical and emotional harm can be caused if the play exercises are forced by eager expectations or too little prior water experience *together*.

Underwater Preparation

Preparation for underwater play is as important for you as it is for baby, so please read Chapters 3 and 11. Let baby stand on your knees or hold onto the wall while you remove her tubie suit. By bracing your back against a pool wall or corner of the pool, you can help to stabilize your own balance. Place your knees together and sit down, so that the thighs, from the hips to the knees, form a fairly flat surface for baby to stand upon (photo 10.1). If you want, you can swing your knees close to the wall where she can hold on at the gutterline or deck until she gets the hang of it.

10.1. Brace your back against the wall of the pool and bring your knees up so that baby has a flat surface on which to stand.

Baby should have ample experience with the tubie suit, but the balance will be somewhat different now without it, and it will take time for her to make adjustments in balance. Should baby sit down suddenly and let go at the wall and go under or slip sideways or backward into the water, retrieve her headfirst and watch for "cues." Babies who recover without tears are ready for occasional underwater dips, but, remember, children who are too surprised or who have difficulty with coughing need more above-water practice.

These dips should be negotiated by your baby by stepping off your legs, sitting down, or letting go of the wall.

As baby adjusts and becomes confident, you can vary your support. Have her stand on the pool steps, the ladder, or a platform in the water. Toys are helpful to encourage baby to reach away, lose her balance, and take a shallow dunking.

When baby adjusts to these initial short and shallow dunkings, you can begin to add variations. In your sitting position, with baby standing upon your thighs, you can stand up. Let her hold onto your arms or balance as best she can, with her chest between your forearms. Wait until baby is standing and balanced (you will feel even pressure from both feet upon your thighs). Before standing yourself (photo 10.2), pull your arms directly to the side, removing your support, and gently raise your hips two to three inches in the water by standing.

10.2. Once you feel the even pressure of both feet on your thighs, you can begin to stand up.

Your once-level thighs will now be on an incline and baby will slip forward or backward slowly, depending upon whether she is facing you or away from you. Continue to stand while she slips off and under by her own body weight. Her face should go underwater over the eyes. Then step forward and retrieve her from behind. As you lift her headfirst from the water, turn her to face you and then hold her chest-to-chest close (photo 10.3).

10.3. After your child slides off your thighs, reach forward, turn him to face you, and hold him chest-to-chest close.

Passes

With a partner you can play passes. Partners face one another in the water about three feet apart. Baby stands on one person's knees facing the partner until steadily balanced. As before, remove your support by drawing your arms to each side as you slowly stand. Baby will again slip forward into the water. The attending partner steps forward and lifts baby from the water for a hug and to watch for "cues." If this is acceptable to baby, the exercise can be repeated, increasing the distance a little each time.

If you feel particularly awkward with these movements and their timing, you may want to try one pass during each water time to allow baby to adjust. If baby anticipates the exercise and begins to cling, you may want to practice passes with baby in his tubie suit. This keeps the game going, helping to keep sensations of balance and loss of balance fresh, but offers baby greater support and confidence. Passes in tubie suits will be above water, of course.

Pulling Underwater

By the time your child is tall enough to use her spine as a lever to pull her head from the water, she'll have the freedom and control to feel comfortable being underwater.

At this time, your child will begin jumping and rolling and throwing her body into the water. Watch what she's doing and see if you can create as many variations as possible for her.

Experienced underwater swimmers will want to learn to extend their underwater time and can be found pulling themselves under at ladders and steps. You can help by counting the seconds while your child is submerged (photo 10.4).

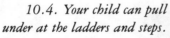
10.4. Your child can pull under at the ladders and steps.

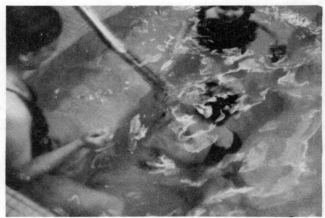

Surface Dives

By the time your baby is pulling under and wanting to extend his time underwater, you can help by positioning his body so that the head and shoulders go under first, forward and below the hips and feet. This takes a lot of practice, and your child may accept your help in going under on this one.

Sinkable toys are an encouragement, and many games can be created around their retrieval (photo 10.5).

10.5. Surface dives are achieved initially by pulling under headfirst.

Goggles can be appropriately introduced at this time. As soon as your child catches on that he can "see" underwater, goggles will become standard swim gear (photos 10.6 and 10.7). Goggles should fit snugly but not make deep red circles around the eyes. Look for goggles with thick, soft padding around the eyes. Elastic head straps are more comfortable than rubber and are easier for the children to handle in putting them on themselves. Fogging up of lenses can be prevented by using any of the antifog products available. Although many competitive swimmers spit in their goggles to reduce fogging, your child will have trouble performing that task. Defogging your baby's goggles with your own saliva is not recommended. All saliva carries bacteria and germs, and this practice would increase the risk of your child developing an eye infection.

10.6. At this time, a child becomes interested in seeing underwater, and goggles open up a whole new world.

10.7. Dancing with his mother, Nicholas submerges to keep an eye on our cameraman.

In supporting the Water Play philosophy of trust and sharing, underwater work follows two strict rules:

1. Adult hands *always lift* baby up and to the surface of the water where there is light, air, and familiar and reassuring faces.
2. Baby will go under the water on his own power and by the force of his own body weight. This means that you cannot pull or push baby underneath the water surface (see section on Water Intoxication in Chapter 11), nor can you throw baby into the water or hold him and jump in (see section on Jumping from Heights, also in Chapter 11).

The pressure that we feel when we are submerged is caused by the difference between the internal pressures in our body's air spaces and the external pressure of the water. The pressure that we as adults feel at a five-foot depth will be much less than what baby feels, because baby's internal air spaces (lungs, sinuses, and ears) are smaller.

Because your infant's skeletal system is cartilaginous, and therefore more pliable than an adult's, underwater pressures will cause compression of the rib cage, which will, in turn, compress the lungs. Babies cannot equalize those pressures by themselves. We actually have very little understanding of the physiology of diving and underwater submersions for infants and toddlers. But because the infant's sensory system is operating wide open, the "feeling" of submersion being a total body experience could be extremely frightening without prior step-by-step preparation and experience.

Until further research can give us better guidelines, we must respect underwater play by allowing baby to have as much control as possible and to submerge *only* by his own movement and body weight and to jump from no greater height than his own body height.

11
Medical Considerations

The Mammalian Diving Reflex

The mammalian diving reflex is a product of our species development, but it is not necessarily associated with water. Predatory animals can close off the back of the throat, completely separating the respiratory-olfactory system from the cavity of the mouth. This allows the animal to grasp prey tightly between clenched teeth while breathing and to be able to smell the approach of its own predators while feeding. It is this same reflex that allows your infant to swallow liquids and breathe at the same time. Essentially it is this reflex that is responsible for the holding of the breath when your newborn gets her face wet.

As mentioned in Chapter 3, the diving reflex is not fully understood, but we do know that newborns will hold their breath when their faces are submerged in water. We also know that between the age of three and six months, this reflex weakens and then disappears for awhile.

To better understand the newborn's breath-holding reflex, you will want to look at the anatomical development of your baby, as well as the physiological components of the reflex.

Structural Placement of the Epiglottis

During early infancy, the epiglottis separates the upper respiratory tract from the upper digestive tract. This is actually a structural separation caused by the physical placement of the epiglottis in relationship to the palate. This structural arrangement provides a continuous airway from the nose through the larynx and into the trachea. This arrangement causes all infants to breathe through their noses (obligate nasal breathing), until the maturational descent of the epiglottis. Babies can breathe through the mouth (oral "tidal," or quiet, respiration), only after the descent of the epiglottis, which occurs between the fourth and sixth months.

Apnea and Bradycardia

The diving reflex involves not only the respiratory system but also the cardiovascular system. It is thought that submerging the facial area around the nostril and sinus cavities triggers the vegus nerve complex to close off the back of the throat and, as a result, breathing ceases (apnea). When your infant is submerged, complex chemical changes occur in the blood. The action of the heart slows down (bradycardia), which in turn increases oxygen extraction from the blood. While submerged, your infant's oxygen demands will decrease, bringing about a redistribution of blood flow and maintenance of arterial pressure. Bradycardia is induced partly because, submerged, your infant has ceased momentarily to breathe and partly from stimulation of nerve endings on the body by being submerged.

Bradycardia can be induced by just submerging the face in water, and, it seems, the colder the water the more quickly the heart begins to slow. Cardiologists use cold-water facial immersions in treating certain spasms of the heart (PMT).

So, the mammalian diving reflex primarily involves the placement of the infant's epiglottis in the throat and his breathing through the nose. Stimulation of the reflex by submersion causes the epiglottis to close off the back of the throat and the breathing to stop. Submersion also decreases the system's oxygen needs, so the heart slows. Because breathing has ceased, chemical changes within the blood increase oxygen extraction from the blood. Because this reflex is so complex and because the respiratory and cardiovascular systems' exchange is so finely balanced, it is not easy to say what actually first triggers the reflex. But over the years we have discovered a serious problem with the reliability of the reflex and, therefore, with the immersion techniques that are taught in many infant swimming programs.

Water Intoxication

Pediatricians have recently encountered babies with health problems caused by swallowing enough water to severely lower sodium serum levels of their blood. This results in a variety of symptoms, the most severe of which leads to convulsions and death. These case studies point not only to the fact that these were "older" babies, but also to the fact that in each incidence the baby was being "helped" to swim.

In various programs, babies are "helped" to submerge or are forcefully pushed under and through the water (torpedoed). Many parents have been taught to blow into their babies' faces and then pull them underneath the surface of the water. The feeling is like hanging your head out of the car window. It takes your breath away. But although you can draw your head back in the window, your baby has no control at all. This violates our standards of trust and offering baby the opportunity to make choices. Additionally, if baby is in midbreath when you begin to blow into his face, the likelihood of his inhaling water increases dramatically. You should be aware that if you weigh 150 pounds, a ten-pound baby will weigh only 6.6% of your total body weight. By grasping your baby by the back of the neck and pushing him under and then through the water, his back is forced to arch at the neck. Whenever the back arches at the neck, the mouth drops open. While baby is torpedoing forward through the water, water is naturally forced into the open cavity.

Since nature has made it difficult for your baby to breathe in water, the only option is to swallow the water. Even tiny babies with strong diving reflexes and also older, stronger babies would not necessarily have the strength to withstand such pressure forcing water into the back of the throat. Again, because of individual differences in body weight and the strength of the reflexive response, the amount of ingested water that will cause these problems varies. In almost every instance of water intoxication or pediatric drowning that occurs in a supervised class environment these two techniques were being taught by a certified instructor. The truly tragic aspect of this type of instruction is that it is usually the parent who, in all faith and with the best of intentions, unwittingly inflicts the damage upon his own infant.

Babies who are allowed to encounter the water with only the force that their own body weight exerts will be far less susceptible to water intoxication and associated problems.

Parents who want to work with their newborns in water at home will want to concentrate on their infant's developmental levels and use water as a medium to enhance creatively their babies' development.

Healthy Water

Swimming pool water, even in those pools filled from city taps, needs to be chemically treated for impurities. Bathing bodies and environmental dirt in suspended or dissolved solids leave biological materials that need to be removed through circulation of the water through filters. Bacteria and algae grow quickly in a teaching pool, where water is maintained between 86° and 92° F. Chemicals must be checked and added more frequently than in pools kept at lower water temperatures.

PH levels should remain between 7.2 and 7.6. When the pH level falls below 7.2, the water becomes acidic. Acidic water not only causes corrosion in all metal filtration and plumbing parts, but also logically alters or practically destroys the pH mantle on human skin. Eye infections, athlete's foot, and assorted types of fungi and dermatitis are the most general complaints of devoted swimmers.

Pediatricians have recently reported dental caries and aching teeth, which have yellowed or became translucent and loose in young patients who swim regularly in pools containing acidic water.

Diaper rashes as well as bumps and scrapes sometimes appear to be helped by a good soaking, but heavily chlorinated water can cause visible irritation. Common sense will get us through the scraped knees and infectious skin rashes, such as poison ivy, but when in doubt, you should consult your pediatrician.

Ear Infections

Because an infant's ear canal is short and straight, water entering the canal can push bacteria growing in the warmth of the canal into the middle ear. Some infants are particularly prone to ear problems throughout infancy, but then grow out of them as the structure of the canal angles and elongates. Earplugs may help keep water out of the ears, but they, too, can force existing bacteria from the canal into the middle ear. Swimming just might not be the most practical sport for these little ones. A series of ear infections can lower your infant's resistance to disease, and at a time when growth occurs so rapidly, the added stress of continuous infections can hold back your infant's development. Swimming can be tried again in a year.

Jumping and Diving from Heights

Although we have little research on the diving reflex in infants, we have even less on babies jumping and diving from decks and from low and high boards. Infants and babies are not miniature adults. Structurally and developmentally they are vastly different even from a four-year-old. And we have no research on height recommendations for diving four-year-olds.

As when they balance on land, babies and children in water need spinal length to balance the weight of the head. Toddlers and children who are "head heavy" on land and in the water will also be "head heavy" in the air. The greater the height of the jump, the more likely your child is going to hit the water in an awkward position. Should the head hit first, the neck may be injured by whiplash. The damage to a growing spinal column cannot be ascertained. The risk is too great.

The impact of a small body hitting the water surface forcefully or from a height can tear ligaments that support internal organs in the abdominal cavity, displacing organs. Internal organs have also ruptured upon impact. Body cavities, such as the ears, eyes, sinuses, rectum, and vagina can also be permanently damaged by water forced into them upon impact.

Trust Your Intuition

Parents who want their babies to swim make quite an investment in personal time, effort, and money for the classes and equipment. Instructors who coach infant aquatics classes do so because they love children and like being with them. Teachers and parents also believe that they are providing a unique service that will have a lifelong impact upon the lives of their young charges, and this makes infant swimming immensely rewarding work.

Understanding what your child is capable of accomplishing in the water is a complicated process. Research in the field of infant aquatics will help us in developing realistic expectations for our children in the water environment, but this will take years to pull together and implement.

What can we do now to protect babies and to make swimming for even the youngest infant a safe yet enjoyable learning experience? *Develop empathy with your child.*

If he is hesitant or fearful, look for reasons *why.* Once you have a reason you can find an acceptable solution. Then, no matter what type program you enroll in, you can work within safe boundaries. If he screams because he's been pushed underneath the water, accept his screams as his only way of telling you that he was absolutely terrified and even angered by the experience. The rationale offered in many programs that this is good for him discourages sensitive communication and increases the risk for emotional and physical trauma.

Should you already have developed a fair amount of empathy with your child, and another adult (whether it be a close relative or a class instructor) encourages you to continue an exercise that your child definitely doesn't like, *follow your child's cues.* If you are still pressured to conform, pick up your child and leave.

12
Flotation Aids and Aquatic Gear

A dults and young children alike enjoy floating in water. Gentle rocking motions relax tired bodies. Babies, too, can be lulled to sleep in water and need constant supervision even with inflatable toys. How suitable flotation aids or aquatic toys are for your baby depends upon the individual capabilities of your baby, the recommended usage or the manufacturer's instructions, the amount of close adult participation in your baby's water activity, and the water area itself (ocean, lake, or swimming pool).

Babies are often unwilling to put something strange on or over their heads, so before having your baby use any type of aquatic gear, play with the item at home first. You can also just leave the item on the pool deck for your child to discover. After several play sessions with the item, and the opportunity to play with it and chew on it, most likely it will end up in the water. Several attempts will probably need to be made before your baby will actually wear the item or use it correctly. But your baby may discover uses for an item that you couldn't have imagined. Never force a new toy or swimming aid upon a baby.

Flotation Aids

There are three types of flotation aids, PFDs (personal flotation
devices approved by the Coast Guard), inflatable aquatic toys,
and swimming aids.

PFDs are used primarily for boating. Several models are spe-
cifically designed for use by infants and babies and have special
collars that are to help keep a baby's head above water. Although a good idea, PFDs are hampered by the fact that one
size fits all. One size will fit each baby differently, and in order
to ensure that the vest or jacket works properly, it is imperative
that it fit properly. Realistically, your baby may outgrow a vest
in less than three or four months. The same jacket cannot be
used two summers for the same child or even held as an acceptable hand-me-down for a younger sibling, so the expense is
great. Boating is an especially hazardous activity for toddlers
and infants, so if boating is a big part of your family's summers, make sure you make safety your number one consideration. Check with your local Coast Guard for their
recommendations, call your local boating or diving shop, or
write for their catalogue of PFDs.

Inflatable aquatic toys include inner tubes (some with seats)
and arm bands. Inflatable tubes or donuts generally encircle
baby and rely upon her to extend her arms over the sides, resting her body weight on top. This limits arm action, and some
babies will still have an operable startle (moro) reflex and,
should they be surprised by a sudden noise or splash, will lift
both arms; and possibly slip through the encircling tube.

Inner tubes will hold baby in a vertical position in the water,
but babies are head heavy and their bodies are short. The
amount of body underneath the water is not enough to stabilize
baby on the surface of the water. Tipping too far in any direction can cause the inner tube or seat to flip upside down, with
baby still inside. Babies of all ages have been known to rest
their chins upon the front of the circle and then decided to taste
it. With gravity pushing baby's body weight down upon the

tube, it will rapidly deflate with even one puncture from a sharp little tooth.

Inflatable arm bands also simulate the vertical position, but restrict baby's use of the arms, limiting exploration and muscular development. Arm bands are normally worn close to the shoulders and, while baby is resting, invite thoughtful chewing. Just like the inner tube, the arm bands will deflate rapidly with a small puncture. Older babies who are extremely active can also lose an arm band while playing.

Swimming aids range from eggs or cubes that strap around the baby's back and chest to buoyant tank suits. Although they all help baby simulate a nearly vertical position in the water, the egg or cube can ride up on baby's back, pushing against the back of the head, forcing baby's face down and toward the water. This is uncomfortable and often times threatening. The strap on the egg or cube often rises up underneath the arms, chafing tender skin. Care should be taken initially to adjust the strap and to keep it snug. Elastic straps will stretch and rot and will need to be replaced periodically. Nylon straps can be taken in and stitched down (with the extra fabric to the outside to prevent chafing), to be let out as baby grows. The strap itself can be slipped through a band of soft fabric to prevent chafing.

Tubie suits are unisex tank suits in which oblong pockets are stitched around the chest and back. Polyethylene or Styrofoam tubes are then inserted into these pockets. The suit helps baby simulate the vertical position. It frees the arms, and the tubes can be removed one at a time in a balanced fashion from the front as well as the back pockets. This allows baby the opportunity of assuming control of his buoyancy as respiratory and muscular strength develop. Tubie suits allow for reduced water buoyancy if used correctly and encourage your baby's independence. As your baby grows confident and competent in buoyancy skills, there will actually come a time when he experiences the aid as a cumbersome thing that slows down his activity and reduces the tactile reinforcement from the water. It is at this point that your child will ask to take the suit off or actually refuse to wear it.

There are a few variations on the original tubie suit from England called the Polyotter. The Ero Industries suit has a front and back pouch into which flat foam slabs fit. This foam has the texture of dolphin flesh when wet and is quite nice to touch. Aqua Learn produces a tubie suit as well as a vest with an inflatable tube around the waist. The buoyancy of all the flotation suits varies because of the difference in the cut of the suit and the buoyancy materials.

Aquatic Gear

Flippers, goggles, and even swim caps are supposed to be designed to increase speed, vision, and water comfort. Aquatic gear for infants, however, is often uncomfortable to wear, and comfort should be your primary consideration in making a purchase. No matter how good an idea it may be, if the item hurts or is uncomfortable, your baby will not consent to wear it.

Flippers are useful for any age. They should be made of soft, pliable rubber or plastic with narrow ankle straps. We often cut the straps down and file down rough edges. Longer flippers are more suitable for infants and toddlers because they are heavier, pulling the knees straight and down, thereby extending baby's own body length and creating greater stability for babies who are learning balance and stability skills. The flip part of flippers can be cut down for independent babies who are developing speed, or shorter flippers can be purchased.

Kickboards are ideal for water play as well as for serious swimming. Look for the densely packed, heat-treated kickboards because your baby will love to bite this particular piece of equipment. You will find hundreds of little teeth marks in the board in a very short period of time, but small children cannot bite hunks out of the denser, heat-treated boards. Child-size kickboards will be easier for your little one to manage in the water.

Two kickboards, one held underneath each arm in the water, become water wings. We often have little water angels with toy halos upon their heads swim with us. A kickboard also acts as a stability device once baby gets the hang of keeping her feet behind her. Once kicking begins, children like to pile toys upon their kickboard "boats" and ferry them across the pool to unload them on the other side.

Swim caps are not really necessary for most babies, but older babies who have hair long enough to get into their eyes may want to try a cap. Caps are made of rubber or lycra, like the competitive swim suits. Whichever you purchase, the cap should fit snugly, but not leave marks around baby's head. Rubber caps tend to pull hair and they really won't keep water out of the baby's ears. Lycra caps are more comfortable to wear. Although they are a bit more expensive, they can be worn for several seasons, if you don't lose them. Since adult heads and baby heads are close to the same size, you might just want to loan your baby yours.

Goggles are alien to babies and most just don't like them. Goggles change familiar faces to near monsters and are unfamiliar to wear, fitting around the eyes and head. Most children won't wear goggles until they find that they can see under water with them (at about three to four years).

There is no practical reason for an infant to wear goggles, but toddlers will be interested in looking them over. Once goggles have been demonstrated, you can help baby to hold them up to his eyes. Later you can loosely fit the band around his head to hold them on. Goggles that are too tight can place undue pressure upon the eyeball itself. Babies should not be allowed to jump or dive into the water with goggles on because of the added pressure that impact will place upon the eyes. Goggles should not be pushed down over the ears and left loosely hanging around the neck while baby is involved in water play. Goggles worn around the neck while baby is swimming can get caught or just float to the water surface and interfere with rythmic breathing. Goggles left dangling around baby's neck while he jumps can damage teeth and cause facial lacerations and bruises.

An interesting thing to note with your own child is that upon surfacing while wearing goggles, he will not breathe in until the goggles are lifted off the eyes to the forehead or removed. So, the first thing you will generally find is that your baby will reach for the goggles right away (just as babies submerged up to the eyes assume they are above water and will breathe in). This is normal and will disappear later. For maximum comfort, choose goggles with elastic straps and wide, round lenses ("fish eye") that are heavily padded.

Goggles can be "tried on" by holding one lens at a time up to baby's eye. Lightly press the rubber foam against the bony circle around the eye. If the lens momentarily stays because of suction, you have a good seal. Try the same thing with the other lens on the other eye. Remember that the nose piece will initially be stiff and may change the suction of the lenses until it is broken in. Nose pieces should be adjusted to the bridge of baby's nose and the excess clipped off. Be sure to round all edges so that no rough surfaces scratch and pinch the nose.

Goggles come with a variety of tinted lenses to reduce or increase the amount of light in the water. Children swimming indoors should begin with untinted lenses to avoid perceptual distortions.

Face masks present special problems and are not recommended for preschoolers. Even older children (three to five years) attempt to breath through the nose underwater with the face mask on and they seem to have difficulty breathing through the mouth with the face mask on while above water. These problems are associated with the vestibular system and the diving reflex.

Much familiarization time is needed with goggles and face masks and shallow surface diving before these difficulties can be voluntarily corrected by your child. Your own continued use of goggles will offer the greatest encouragement for your child to use goggles.

Nose clips are not practical for preschoolers because of the problems associated with the diving reflex and because their use prevents controlling breath through the nose underwater.

Ear plugs change and distort pool sounds but are okay to use. Most babies will pull at the ear and dislodge them, but parents with babies who are susceptible to ear infections may want to try them as a last resort (see Chapter 10).

New aquatic toys and equipment are being developed each year. In making any purchase, consider the intended purpose of the item and whether you would really use it for that purpose. Is the item's design practical for its intended use? For example, if you are purchasing a swimming aid, can you reduce the item's buoyancy? Are the materials from which the item is made non-toxic and bitable yet resistant to having holes bitten in it or hunks taken out of it? Is the item well constructed from durable materials or is it just a two-day investment?

Doting grandparents usually don't mind a $30 weekend investment, but do *you?* Consider where the item will be used most (public or private pool) and consider whether or not the item is safe for use by children of different ages. For safe aquatic play, remember that each child will need constant supervision in and near water, even with additional swimming aids.

Aquatic Manufacturers

Tubie suits or similar tank suit flotation aids can be ordered from the following outlets. You can write or call these manufacturers for their catalog or the name of their retail distributor in your hometown.

Aqua Leisure Industries
Avon Industrial Park
P.O. Box 25
Avon, MA 02322
(617) 587-5400

Polyotter Floatsuit
Marnin, Incorporated
P.O. Box 128
Freehold, NJ 07728

(Marnin, Incorporated is the United States distributor for the English-made Pollyotter float suit. Please write as there is no listed number. In my opinion, the Pollyotter suit is the best made for balance and durability, and well worth the extra time required to order.)

Goggles, flippers, kickboards, swim caps, and face masks can be ordered from these companies:

Ero Industries, Incorporated
5940 West Touhy Avenue
Chicago, IL 60648
(312) 647-0700
(800) 323-5999
East Coast Sales Office:
(201) 238-6541

The Finals
21 Minisink Avenue
Port Jervis, NY 12771
(800) 431-9111

Hind-Wells, Incorporated
390 Buckley Road
San Luis Obispo, CA 93401
(805) 235-4150
(800) 235-4150 (outside CA)

National Aquatic Service
1425 Erie Boulevard East
Syracuse, NY 13210
(315) 479-5544 (call collect in NY State)
(800) 448-5521 (outside NY State)

Speedo
5203 S.E. Johnson Creek Boulevard
Portland, OR 97222
(800) 547-4601 (Western U.S.)
(800) 547-4687 (Eastern U.S.)

The Swim Shop
1400 8th Avenue South
P. O. Box 1402
Nashville, TN 37203
(800) 251-1412

Uglies Unlimited
1617 East Highland
Phoenix, AZ 85016
(800) 528-3650

World Wide Aquatics
509 Wyoming Avenue
Cincinnati, OH 45215
(800) 543-4459

Toys are as much a delight to us as to our children. Educational and developmental toys serve purposes greater than entertainment and diversion and should be chosen with care. Select an array of floatable *and* sinkable toys for your water area. Call or write for the following toy company catalogues.

ChildCraft
20 Kilmer Road
Edison, NJ 08817
(800) 631-5657

The First Years
1 Kiddie Drive
Avon, MA 02322
(800) 225-0382 or (617) 588-1220

Fisher-Price
606 Girard Street
East Aurora, NY 14052
(716) 687-3000
(800) 828-7315

Johnson & Johnson Child Development Toys
6 Commercial Street
Hicksville, NY 11801
(516) 433-4672 or (800) 645-7470

Toys "R" Us
300 Distribution Circle
Suite A
Fairfield, OH 45014
(513) 874-8844

Safety equipment for home tub and sink use is essential. Follow your manufacturer's guidelines and keep your baby under constant supervision for safe bathing. Faucet covers, no-slip tread strips, and other bathing necessities can be found in the baby furniture section of your local toy and department stores.

A catalogue of the wonderful water music that we use and that the babies love can be ordered from:

Halpern Sounds
c/o Grama Vision Records
260 West Broadway, New York, NY 10013
(800) 845–4848

Dr. Halpern, Ph.D., is director of Spectrum Research Institute and a pioneer in the field of sound health.

13
Choosing a Class

A s infant aquatics classes become increasingly popular, you will probably find several facilities in your city that offer infant classes. The more you know about infant aquatics, the better the decision you can make in choosing a program for you and your baby. The yellow pages of your telephone book and also local parents' directories will list the locations and phone numbers of private and public pool facilities in your city.

Phone Ahead

Parents' groups will usually have information on programs. The YMCA, the Water Safety Department of the American Red Cross, and your pediatrician will have information, but word-of-mouth recommendations are your best assurance of quality instruction. Plan to visit as many programs as practically possible before enrolling. Phone the facility ahead of time to make arrangements for your visit. Any facility that will not allow prospective students (parents and babies) to visit a class prior to enrolling should be immediately crossed off your list. Most facilities will assign someone to speak to you and show you through the facility. Other facilities will hold open houses for groups of prospective parents to watch children in the water. Program philosophies and methods of water instruction should be explained and all questions should be answered.

Take Baby

Take baby with you on your visits. Baby's reactions to a facility will be helpful to you in making your decisions.

What is the size of the class? In observing a program, look to see if most of the babies are happy or distressed. Observe how much individual attention is given to each baby and parent.

Time

Time considerations will include commuting time and available parking as well as class times offered. If you must change your child's routine to attend class, remember to allow several weeks for baby to make the necessary adjustments.

Environmental Concerns

You'll be carrying bulky towels and swimming gear along with the usual diaper paraphernalia. The added bulk often is just enough to tip your balance, so you will both be safer with a facility with few or no stairs. Is there adequate room for parking strollers, heavy winter coats, and soaking wet umbrellas? Do you have to stop and rearrange weight and girth to enter the doors to the facility? Are there stairs between the locker rooms and pool area?

Sensory Considerations

Are the pool and locker room and the equipment clean and pleasing to the eye? Consider noise levels; are echoes too loud or will your class follow a large, noisy, children's group? Consider odors. Is there a "mildew" smell or a heavy moist chlorine odor? Is there good ventilation in the locker rooms and pool areas? Do you feel at ease or slightly claustrophobic?

Consider touch. Are the locker room and pool area floors cold and slippery when wet? Are these areas warm or drafty? Are shower sprays too harsh for baby's skin? Is the pool water invitingly warm (86° F minimum) or does it "chill" you to think about getting in?

Look for Consistency

In choosing a program, look for consistency among the physical environment, the program philosophy, and the method of instruction that is employed in teaching that philosophy.

Developmentally oriented programs will provide all environmental factors necessary for safe and comfortable water exercises and an exceptionally long adjustment time to the water. Water exercises should offer each child the opportunity to use and strengthen muscles as well as practice in decision making.

Program Philosophy

What is the philosophy of the program? Are the instructional methods used in the water consistent with the program philosophy? Does your infant respond favorably to the instruction? Any program may claim to be developmentally sound, but may use stimulus-response methods of water training (such as forced immersions for babies).

Any program that does not allow baby to make choices or decisions is not considerate of her emotional reactions and is not a developmental program.

Program Instructors

In the history of infant swimming, physical educators, recreation instructors, swimming instructors, or parents with an interest have developed methods of instruction simply through trial and error. Experimentation has generally followed an intuitive process. Methods have been selectively applauded or booed by friends and neighbors, with local followings gradually developing. As a result, infant aquatic programs of varying quality "splashed" up all across the United States. Consequently, we are now concerned with the teaching of thousands of infants and babies under the age of three by teachers who are not always adequately trained.

In the United States, in order to be employed or to volunteer at a camp, club, or public facility as an instructor of infant aquatics, one must hold a current American Red Cross or YMCA Senior Life Saving Certificate and be currently certified as a Water Safety Instructor. The American Red Cross, however, follows the recommendation of the Council for National Cooperation in Aquatics, which states that the minimum age for organized swimming be set at age three. The Red Cross, therefore, does not offer material on infant aquatics in its instructor certification programs. Although the American Medical Association does not recommend an organized program of swimming instruction for children under the age of three years, the National YMCA has recently stated that it "recognizes the opportunities for the child, parent, and YMCAs in aquatics programs for the child under three years of age." Amid conflicts of interest and intended well-being, infant aquatics programs are still being conducted. Their potential is handicapped by the fact that there are no standardized, recognized methods for the teaching of instructors of infant aquatics, because there are no outlined methods for the instruction of parent and baby in a recognized infant aquatics program.

It would be advantageous if more child development and medical professionals would be interested in instructing infant aquatics classes, even on a part-time basis. But until we estab-

lish interest with child care professionals or develop standardized methods of instruction, you will want to ask the following
questions of any potential program instructor.

1. What prior land experience does the instructor have with
   infants, toddlers, and preschoolers?
2. What prior experience does the instructor have with infants,
   toddlers, and preschoolers in the water?
3. What prior experience does the instructor have in teaching
   other water activities?
4. Is the instructor's previous water experience based in a competitive swimming background (in general, a competitive
   swimmer will be more goal-oriented)? Or was the instructor's
   experience primarily in leisurely or recreational aquatics?
5. Does the instructor have a background in early childhood
   development?
6. Does your child respond favorably to the instructor?

Consider the instructor's relationship with the facility. Often
the instructor has very high standards for the program but is
unable to implement them. For example, adult membership
using the pool for lap swims will need cooler water temperatures. To raise the water temperature to accommodate the
babies would cause a problem for the lap swimmers. This is a
no-win situation that can be bypassed only by looking for a
facility that works with both the physically handicapped and
senior-citizen groups. All three groups require warmer water
and air temperatures. Better yet, look for a facility with a separate teaching pool.

Trust Your Intuition

Because water is such a tactile and expressive environment, our
response to minute changes in the ever-changing currents becomes immediate. This natural response seems to bypass the

world of reason and logic and appears strictly intuitional. Cultivate your intuition. Take time to watch and observe and experience the smallest and most subtle sensations. Your child's response to the water will be even more immediate than your own. Watch your child and learn from him. Observe small changes in his balance and water maneuverings. Cultivate your intuition and trust your child's intuition.

Concessions

Once you have visited several facilities, choose the one you and baby feel most comfortable with. Consider all individual preferences and know that there will always be concessions. You may have to drive across town to attend a program that offers a more consistent developmental program than the one offered just down the street.

You may opt for the program with the least experienced instructor because the facility maintains warmer pool water, or you may choose the older facility with the broken windows because the instructor is highly qualified. Whatever the concessions, you will feel more confident in your decision because you actively sought all alternatives before making your decision. You will be relaxed and confident (and able to learn more in the water because you are confident) that you have chosen the best program available to you.

Checklist for Choosing a Class

This checklist is designed to help you locate the most supportive and sound program available to you.

Mark your answers to the questions in the appropriate yes/no boxes at the right-hand side of the page. Put a question mark beside those questions for which you cannot decide on an answer.

After you finish, tally up your "yes" answers and then the "no's." The facility and program for which you answered the most "yes's" will be the one that will provide you and your baby with the most supportive environment for your water play.

If two programs tally up close in "yes's," look at each different category, like Pool Area, Program, etc., and then tally those "yes's" according to category. One program may be deficient in facilities but shine in programming. You can then decide what is more important to you and your baby.

Should you find you have more question marks than "yes" or "no" answers for a particular facility and its program, it may mean that you need to take more time to tour the facility and ask questions.

Take as much time as you need now to get to know the facility, its program, its philosophy, and the methods of instruction that are employed.

Good-natured persistence will pay off for you and your baby, as well as the facility, because once you choose a program after judging alternatives, you will be more content with your decision and learn more in the classes.

Name/Address of Facility _____

_____

Telephone # _____

FIRST THINGS FIRST

	YES	NO
1. Do the instructors take time on the phone to explain their program philosophy and teaching techniques?		
2. Does this facility allow you to observe classes before enrolling?		
3. Does this facility have a separate "teaching" pool or maintain water temperature at a minimum of 86°F?		
4. Do parents attend their babies in the classes?		
TOTAL:		

YOUR FIRST VISIT

Round-trip mileage: _____

Round-trip travel time: _____

Parking expense: $ _____

Tuition cost of program: $ _____

	YES	NO
1. Is the street entrance on the same level with the sidewalk (no stairs)?		
2. Are the street doors easy to maneuver with strollers and bulky bags?		
3. Once inside, is there adequate room to safely park strollers?		
4. Is there adequate and secure space for heavy winter coats, wet umbrellas, and boots?		
5. Is there a lounge area or play area where children can roam safely while you are checking in?		

TOTAL: _____

LOCKER ROOMS

	YES	NO
1. Are the locker room areas pleasing to the eye?		
2. Are the locker rooms clean?		
3. Are the locker rooms adequately ventilated—no heavy chlorine vapors or musty odors?		
4. Does water drain easily from floor surfaces?		
5. Are locker room areas comfortably warm?		
6. Are shower handles out of reach of your child?		
7. Check shower sprays. Are they soft enough for baby's skin?		

TOTAL: _____

POOL AREA

	YES	NO
1. Do locker room doors enter into the pool area at the shallow end of the pool?		
2. Is there adequate deck space for you to leisurely prepare to enter the water?		
3. Is the pool area pleasing to the eye?		
4. Do deck surfaces drain well?		
5. Is the pool water maintained at 86° F minimum?		
6. Are air temperatures comfortable for the wet people you are observing?		
7. Is there relaxing and appropriate "water music" in the pool area?		
8. Are overhead lights softened?		
9. Are more babies in the classes you observed happy rather than distressed?		
10. Does the instructor give each parent and baby individual attention?		

TOTAL: _____

PROGRAM

	YES	NO
1. Does the program philosophy consider each baby's intellectual and emotional development as important as physical development and skill acquisition?		
2. Do the teaching techniques employed in the program support your baby's need for comfort and security?		
3. Do the teaching techniques support the heads up–bottoms under or vertical swimming position for babies?		
4. Do the teaching techniques support baby's learning balance and buoyancy in water through land skills of sitting, standing, and walking?		
5. Do the teaching techniques encourage your baby's independent exploration of balance and buoyancy in the water environment?		

6. Does the program effectively use flotation tank suits (the ones from which the floats can be removed one at a time)?
7. Do the teaching techniques encourage you to do the "coaching" for your baby?
8. Do the teaching techniques *avoid* forced underwater immersions like torpedos and blowing in baby's face and then pulling or pushing baby under?
9. Do the teaching techniques *avoid* having baby jump from a height greater than his own body height?

TOTAL: _____

INSTRUCTOR

YES   NO

1. Does your instructor have prior infant teaching experience?
2. Does your instructor have prior water experience with your baby's age group?
3. Does your instructor have a background in early child development?

TOTAL: _____

INTUITIVELY SPEAKING

YES   NO

1. Intuitively, do you feel good about the program?
2. Intuitively, do you feel good about the instructor?
3. Intuitively, do you feel good about the facility?
4. Was your baby's response to the visit positive?

TOTAL: _____

AFTERTHOUGHTS

In a facility that services many community groups, find out what other classes will be using the pool and locker room facilities before and after the class time that you are interested in. If possible, you will want to avoid scheduling your class before or after a large group of older children or teenagers, because of increased noise and activity levels.

CLASS TIME	INSTRUCTOR	GROUP BEFORE	GROUP AFTER
_____	_____	_____	_____
_____	_____	_____	_____
_____	_____	_____	_____
_____	_____	_____	_____
_____	_____	_____	_____
_____	_____	_____	_____
_____	_____	_____	_____
_____	_____	_____	_____

14
Write to Us

B ecause Water Dancing is just the beginning of an exciting new field of body learning and movement communication, we want you to write to us and let us know how your Water Dancing with your own baby has developed. What do you and your baby enjoy the most? What have you learned about your baby through Water Dancing?

For example, Stacy had just begun walking. As she grew increasingly steady on her feet, the territory that she covered expanded. Upon arriving one morning, Stacy's mother sat her down at the top of the two stairs leading down from the locker room to the pool area. Hand-in-hand they descended into the pool area together. Stacy loved those steps! She climbed up and then back down again and again. She then sat on each step to view the children in the water. Every time her mother picked her up to head for the pool, Stacy threw a fit. I encouraged Stacy's mother to let her "work" on the steps and reluctantly she agreed.

After almost three weeks of no swimming, and at the end of mother's patience with me and Stacy, Stacy abruptly became interested in the water. Except for an extra climb or two at entry and departure to the pool area, Stacy spent her class time in the water. The time she missed in the water was apparent at first in her levels of breath control and buoyancy, but by the end of the session she was swimming along with the others, independent in her tubie suit.

Stacy's mother learned that Stacy's stubbornness was not an attempt to thwart her authority. The experience also helped Stacy's mother to better understand that there would be more developmental interests to unfold as Stacy matured, and that Stacy would put them aside herself at the appropriate time. Stacy's mother also developed a better sense of the time necessary to see Stacy's progress.

As goal-oriented people living in a fast-paced society, we often have a goal-oriented outlook on time and progress. Fortunately, babies have their own goals and they can teach us how to relax and enjoy the "process" of obtaining goals. Your viewpoint as a participating parent is especially important, in helping us understand your expectations of your Water Dancing.

Also, by sending us copies of your "How to Choose a Class" charts, we can better pinpoint areas that need necessary change. As research programs concerning infant aquatics increase, there will be new theories and more detailed information concerning all areas of infant aquatics.

By requesting information updates, we can keep you informed of the latest developments. We realize that we may be deluged with letters, but we promise to answer every request.

So, write to us with your own experiences, your questions, and your observations. You can reach us in care of St. Martin's Press, 175 Fifth Avenue, New York, NY 10010.

Bibliography

Aakhus, T., and Johansen, K. "Angiocardiography of the Duck During Submersion Asphyxia." *Arta Physiol. Scand.* 63: 10–17, 1964.

"Accidental Drownings by Age and Activity." *Statistical Bulletin of the Metropolitan Life Insurance Company,* Vol. 58, May 1977, pp. 2–5.

Als, Heidelise, "Social Interaction: Dynamic Matrix for Developing Behavioral Organization." I. C. Uzgins, ed., *Social Interaction and Communication During Infancy.* New Directions for Child Development, Vol. 40, pp. 21–41. San Francisco: Jossey-Bass, 1979.

——— "The Unfolding of Behavioral Organization in the Face of a Biological Violation." Edward Z. Tronick, ed., *Social Interchange in Infancy.* Baltimore: University Park Press, 1982, pp. 125–159.

Anderson, Harold T. "Physiological Adaptations in Diving Vertebrates." *Physiol. Rev.,* Vol. 46, April 1966, pp. 212–243.

Andrews, C. *Pull-Pull-Kick-Kick: Swimming Lesson Plans for Water Babies and Toddlers.* Shreveport, Louisiana: YMCA, 1975, p. 21.

Aronson, E., and Rosenbloom, S. "Space Perception in Early Infancy: Perception Within a Common Auditory-Visual Space." *Science,* 1971, pp. 1161–1163.

Bates, John E., et al. "Dimensions of Individuality in the Mother-Infant Relationship at Six Months of Age." *Child Development,* Vol. 53, 1982, pp. 446–461.

Beebe, B., and Stern, D. "Engagement-Disengagement and Early Object Experiences," M. Freedman and S. Grand, eds., *Communicative Structures and Psychic Structures.* New York: Plenum Publishing Corp., 1977, pp. 35–55.

Begley, Sharon, and Carey, John. "The Wisdom of Babies." *Newsweek,* January 12, 1981, pp. 71–72.

Bek, William. "What If a Baby Is Born in Water?" *Sputnik,* August 1981, pp. 108–117.

Bell, G. H., and Ribisl, P. M. "Maximal Oxygen Uptake During Swimming of Young Competitive Swimmers 9–17 Years of Age." *Research Quarterly* 50 (4), December 1979, pp. 574–582.

Bergman, S. A., et al. "Diving Reflex in Man: Its Relation to Isometric and Dynamic Exercise." *Journal of Applied Physiol.,* 33, 1972, pp. 27–31.

Betlsworth, M. *Teaching Swimming to Young Children.* New York: Schocken Books, 1980.

Bhatara, V., Clark, D. L., and Arnold, L. E. "Behavioral and Nystagmus Response of a Hyperkinetic Child to Vestibular Stimulation." *The American Journal of Occupational Therapy,* 32, 1978, pp. 311–316.

Bory, Eva. *Teaching Children to Swim.* Sydney, Australia: Hamlyn, 1971.

Bower, T. G. R. *The Perceptual World of the Child.* Cambridge, Massachusetts: Harvard University Press, 1977.

Brazelton, T. B. and Als, H. "Four Early Stages in the Development of Mother-Infant Interaction." *Psychoanalytic Study of the Child,* 34, 1979, pp. 349–369.

Bronson, W. "Mother-Toddler Interaction. A Perspective Studying the Development of Competence," *Merrill-Palmer Quarterly of Behavioral Development,* 20, 1974, pp. 275–301.

Bruneman, C. "Surviving the Swimming Lesson Dilemma." *Day Care and Early Education* 3 (5), May/June 1976, pp. 32–34.

Bruner, J. S., "The Organization of Action and the Nature of the Adult-Infant Translation." Edward Z. Tronick, ed., *Social Interchange in Infancy.* Baltimore: University Park Press, 1982, pp. 23–25.

———"The Organization of Early Skilled Action." *Child Development,* 1973, 44, pp. 1–11.

Clarke, David H. "Effect of Immersion in Hot and Cold Water Upon Recovery of Muscular Strength Following Fatiguing Isometric Exercise." *Archives of Physical Medicine and Rehabilitation,* Vol. 44, October 1953, pp. 565–568.

————and Stelmach, George. "Muscular Fatigue and Recovery Curve Parameters at Various Temperatures." *Research Quarterly,* 37:4, December 1966, pp. 468–479.

Clevenger, D. L., and Gallahue, D. L. Indiana University Developmental Infant Aquatics Laboratory, *Proceedings from the PACE Conference,* Indiana University, Bloomington, Indiana, October 1982, pp. 64–67.

Counsilman, James E. *Competitive Swimming Manual for Coaches and Swimmers.* Bloomington, Indiana: Counsilman Co., Inc., 1977.

Crelin, Edward S. *Development of the Lower Respiratory System.* Clinical Symposia, 27:4, 1975, pub. CIBA Pharmaceutical Co.

————*Development of the Upper Respiratory System.* Clinical Symposia, Vol. 1, 28:2, 1976, pub. CIBA Pharmaceutical Co.

Crowle, L. *Teaching Your Tot to Swim: A Parents' Guide in Ten Progressive Steps.* New York: Vantage Press, 1970.

Deamer, David W. "Music of the Helix: Is There a Musical Message in Our Genes?" *Omni,* August 1982, p. 28.

Deighton, P. "Teaching Deaf Children to Swim," *Swimming Times,* 57:8, 1980, pp. 40–41.

Demarest, S. C. "Movement Responses of Four 3-Month-Old Infants to Prone Submersion." M.S. thesis, University of Madison, Wisconsin, 1979.

Diem, Liselott, "Early Motor Stimulation and Personal Development," *JOPERD,* October 1982, pp. 23–25.

"Don't Baby Your Infants—Teach Them to Swim," *Swimming World* and *Jr., Swimmer,* 19:4. April 1978, p. 33.

Egan, Sean, "Adapting Babies to Water—A Psychological Approach." *New Paths to Sport Learning. Coaching Association of Canada ISSP Fifth World Psychology Congress.* 1978, pp. 101–102.

Elkington, H. *Swimming: A Handbook for Teachers.* Cambridge, England: Cambridge University Press, 1978, p. ix.

————"Teaching Swimming (Part 3) Whole-Part-Whole Method," *Swimming Times,* 57:7, July 1980, pp. 41–42.

Elliott, A. "Principles in Teaching Swimming," *Swimming Times,* 57:1, October 1980, pp. 40–42.

Elsner, R., et al. "Cardiovascular Defense Against Asphyxia," *Science,* 153; 1966, pp. 941–949.

Emde, R., Gaensbauer, T., and Harmon, R., "Emotional Expression in Infancy: A Biobehavioral Study," *Psychological Issues,* 10:37, New York: International Universities Press, 1976.

Ergaugh, S. J. "Assessment of Swimming Performance of Pre-School Children," *Perceptual and Motor Skills,* 47:3, 1978, pp. 1179–1182.

Euler, U. S., Von, et al., "Baroreceptor Impulses in the Carotid Sinus," *Acta Physiol. Scand.,* 1941, pp. 1–9.

Filstrup, Jane Merrill, "In the Swim," *Mothers,* May/June 1980, p. 63.

Foundations of Space Biology and Medicine, M. Calvin, ed., (USA) and O. G. Gazendo, ed. (USSR), Volume II, Books I & II, *Ecological and Physiological Bases of Space Biology and Medicine,* Washington, D.C.: National Aeronautics and Space Administration, 1975.

Freeman, R. K. "The Use of the Oxytocin Challenge Test for Ante-partem Clinical Evaluation of Uteroplacental Respiratory Function," *American Journal of Obstetrical Gynecology,* 1975, pp. 121, 181.

French, James W., et al. "Infant Monkeys—A Model for Crib Death," *American Journal of Diseases of Children,* Vol. 123, May 1972, pp. 480–484.

Gallahue, David L. "Children and Play," *International Association for the Right Child's to Play Conference,* University of Minnesota, April 1983.

——————"Perceptual Aspects of Motor Performance, Motor Development and Kinesiology." Academies at the Minneapolis Conference of AAHPERD, Minneapolis, Minnesota, April 10, 1983.

——————*Understanding Motor Development in Children.* New York: John Wiley and Sons, 1982.

Grasselli, Rose N., and Hegner, Priscilla A., *Playful Parenting.* New York: Putnam Publishing Group, 1981.

Groves, L. *Physical Education for Special Need.* London: Cambridge University Press, 1979.

Haviland, J. "Looking Smart: The Relationship Between Affect and Intelligence." M. Lewis, ed., *Origins of Intelligence.* New York: Plenum Publishing Corp., 1976.

"Help," *Canadian Pool and Patio,* June 1980, pp. 14–16.

Homan, William. "Infants Should Be Wary of Water," *New York Times Magazine,* June 9, 1974.

Houston, Jean, and Masters, Robert. *Listening to the Body.* New York: Dell Publishing, 1978.

Huntinger, P. L., and Donsbach, D. *Water Activities to Enhance Development for Handicapped and High-Risk Infants,* Arlington, Virginia: ERIC, 1980.

Ibuka, Masaru. *Kindergarten Is Too Late,* New York: Simon and Schuster, 1980.

Irving, L. "Bradycardia in Human Divers," *J. Appl. Physiol.,* 18: 489–491, 1963.

Jacobs, B., and Jacobs, I. *Home Pool Safety: A Guide for Parents and Teachers.* Chicago: Nelson-Hall, 1978.

Jaffe, J., and Feldstein, S. *Rhythms of Dialogue.* New York: Academic Press, 1970.

James, L. S. "Biochemical Aspects of Asphyxia at Birth," Adaptation to Extrauterine Life." Rept. 31st Ross Conf. on Ped. Res. T. K. Oliver, Jr., ed. Columbus, Ohio, Ross Laboratories, 1959, pp. 66–71.

Jarvis, M. A. *Enjoy Swimming.* London: Faber, 1972.

Kagan, Jerome. "The Determinants of Attention in the Infant," *American Scientist,* 58:3, May/June 1970, pp. 237–245.

Kingsley, Sir Charles. *The Water Babies.* London: J. M. Dent and Sons, 1957.

Kobayasi, S., and Ogawa, T. "Effect of Water Temperature on Bradycardia During Non-Apneic Facial Immersion in Man," *Jpm. J. Physiol.,* 23, 1973, pp. 613–624.

Kondratyeva, M., and Taborko, V. *Children and Sport in the USSR.* Moscow: Progress Publishers, 1979.

Korop, Peter (Anya Kucharev, trans.). "Path Leading to the Ocean," *Teknika Molodyozhi,* 12, 1979.

Kunx, Kathleen. "To Touch," *Mothers Manual,* November/December 1982, pp. 21–23.

Lawrence, C. C., and Hackett, L. C. *Waterlearning: A New Adventure.* Palo Alto, California: Peek Publications, 1975.

Lewis, Michael, and Michalson, Linda. "What's Your Baby Saying," *Mothers Today,* January/February, 1983, pp. 23–26.

Liedloff, Jean. *The Continuum Concept.* New York: Warner Books, 1977.

Lumby, S. "Another Approach to the Teaching of Beginners," *Swimming Times,* 54:9, September 1977, pp. 22–24.

Manage, M. C. "Reinforced Practice and Reduction of Fear of Water in Children," Ottawa National Library of Canada, M.A. thesis, Louisiana University, 1976.

Matthew, P. K. "Diving Reflex, Clinical Applications of Therapeutic Advances," *Arch. Intern. Med.,* 141, January 1981, pp. 22–23.

McGraw, M. B. "Swimming Behavior of the Human Infant," *J. Pediat.,* 15, 1939, pp. 485–490.

Michaels, R. A., "Philosophical Consideration on Instructional and Competitive Swimming Program Intensity for Younger Children," *Swimming Technique* 16:3, Fall 1979, pp. 95–96.

Miers, E. S., and Lynne, L. *Menehune Majic of How to Swim.* Honolulu: Nakaoi Press, 1967.

Montagu, Ashley. *Touching.* New York: Harper and Row, 1978.

Morna, J. M. "Effects of the Front Crawl Swimming Stroke on Trainable Mentally Retarded Children," Ann Arbor University Microfilms, 1971. Ed.D thesis, University of Utah, 1971.

Morgan, Elaine. *The Aquatic Ape.* London: Souvenir Press Ltd., 1982.

Murphy, M. M. "Pitfalls of Early Swim Lessons," *Journal of Physical Education,* 75:4, 1978, pp. 76–77.

Murray, John L. *Infaquatics,* New York: Leisure Press, 1980.

Nelson, R. "Straddling the Fence on Infant Swimming," *Journal of Physical Education,* 76:1, September/October 1978, p. 20.

Newman, Virginia Hunt. *Teaching an Infant to Swim.* New York: Harcourt Brace Jovanovich, 1967.

Newson, J., and Shotter, J. "How Babies Communicate," *New Society,* 1974, 29, pp. 345–347.

Nixon, J. W., Pearn, H. H., and Dugdale, A. E. "Swimming Ability of Children: A Survey of 4,000 Queensland Children in a High-Drowning Region," *Medical Journal of Australia,* 2:5, 8, September 1979, pp. 271–272.

Oka, H. et al. "Electromyographic and Cinematographic Study of the Flutter Kick in Infants and Children," Conference: International Symposium of Biomechanics in Swimming, 3d, University of Alberta, July 1978, in Perands, J. and Bedingfield, G. W., ed., *Swimming III.* Baltimore: University Park Press, 1979, pp. 167–172.

Olsen, C. R. and Fanestil, D. P. "Effects of Underwater Diving," *J. Applied Physiol.,* 17, 1962, pp. 938–942.

Parker, Donald E. "The Vestibular Apparatus," *Scientific American,* 243, #5, November 1980, pp. 118–135.

Pearce, Joseph Chilton, *Magical Child.* New York: Bantam Books, Inc., 1977.

Pearn, M.D., John, et al. "Prevention of Childhood Drowning Accidents," *Med. J. of Australia,* 1, 1977, pp. 616–618.

Perez, Jim. "Should Babies Swim," *Aquatic World,* 4:5, September 1971, pp. 10–11.

Peterson, P. "Soft Muscles, A Method for Teaching Relaxation in Preschool Swim Classes," *Journal of Physical Education,* 77:3, January 1980, p. 64.

Petsel, P. *Teach Your Tot to Swim.* St. Petersburg, Florida; Great Outdoors, 1974.

Piaget, Jean, and Inhelder, Bärbel. *The Child's Conception of Space.* New York: W. W. Norton and Company, Inc., 1967.

Poe, Pati. "Beginning in the Bathtub," *American Baby,* January, 1980, p. 59.

"Preventing Tragedy: Keeping Your Child Afloat," *Canadian Pool and Patio,* 4:3, Summer 1978.

Prudden, Bonnie. *Your Baby Can Swim.* New York: Reader's Digest Press, 1974.

Ramsey, C. C. "Swimming Behavior of Babies and Young Children," *Swimming Teacher II,* November 1978, pp. 2–4.

Ratov, I. P. "Escape from Gravity," *Teknika Moldyozhi* #3, 1979.

"Rocked Babies Grow Better," *Science Digest,* September 1981.

Rowe, M. I. et al. "Profile of Pediatric Drowning Victims in a Water-Oriented Society," *Journal of Trauma,* 17:8, August 1977, pp. 587–591.

Roy, H. *Swimming and Water-Confidence.* London: Pelham, 1978.

"Russian Babies Learn to Swim," *International Swimmer,* 16:11, February 1980, pp. 3–5.

Schieffelin, J. W. "New Technique in Water Survival Training for Infants and Toddlers," *Pediatric Annals,* 6:11, November 1977, pp. 710–712.

Scholander, P. F. "The Master Switch of Life." *Sci. Am.,* 1963, pp. 209–216.

Sidenbladh, Erik. *Water Babies,* trans. Wendy Croton. New York: St. Martin's Press, 1983.

Skidmore, F. D. "Umbilical Hernia in Child Swimmers," *British Medical Journal,* 2:6188, August 25, 1979, p. 494.

Smith, J. "Swimming for the Under Fives," *Swimming Times,* 54:4, April 1977, pp. 13–16.

Stern, B. "The Goal and Structure of Mother-Infant Play," *Journal of the American Academy of Child Psychology,* 13, 1974a, pp. 4012–4021.

Strauss, M. B. "Physiological Aspects of Mammalian Breath-Hold Diving: A Review," *Aerospace Med.,* 41, 1970, pp. 1362–1381.

Timmermans, Claire, *How to Teach Your Baby to Swim.* New York: Stein and Day, 1981.

Tronick, Edward and Adamson, Lauren. *Babies as People: New Findings on Our Social Beginnings.* New York: MacMillan Publishing Co. Inc., 1980.

Vaccaro, P. "Resting and Exercise Respiratory Function in Well-Trained Child Swimmers," Ann Arbor University, 1977, Ed.D thesis, University of Florida, 1976.

"Water Babies," *Life,* August 6, 1971, p. 56.

"Water Babies," *Newsweek,* April 9, 1962, p. 101.

"Water Babies," *Parents,* June 1981, pp. 70–74.

Webster, S. "Disrobing Movement Education," 75:1, September/October 1977, pp. 10–11.

Weiner, Harvey. *Total Swimming.* New York: Simon and Schuster, 1980.

White, Barton L. *The First Three Years of Life.* New York: Avon Books, 1975.

Widdicombe, J. S. "Respiratory Reflexes in Man," Clinical Science, 21, 1961, pp. 163–170.

————"Reflex Control of Breathing," in MPT, Int. Review of Sci. Physiol., Series one. *Respiratory Physiol.,* 184:2, 1974, pp. 273–301.

Windle, William F. "Brain Damage by Asphyxia at Birth," *Scientific Amer.,* October 1969, pp. 77–84.

Wolf, S. "Bradycardia of Dive Reflex," *Trans. Am. Clin. Climat. Assoc.,* 76, 1964, pp. 192–200.

————"Sudden Death and the Oxygen-Conserving Reflex," *American Heart Journal,* 71, 1966, pp. 840–841.

Index